>> contents

PART ONE: INTERRUPTING HETERONORMATIVITY

FRAMING THE ISSUES

LISTENING TO STUDENTS

ENGAGING NUANCES

PART TWO: RESPONSIBLE PEDAGOGY

PART THREE: LGBT TEACHING RESOURCES

CONTRIBUTORS

>>acknowledgments

T he editors are indebted to the members of the editorial board who initiated and supported this project from inception to print. We thank Margaret Himley, Adrea Jaehnig, and Andrew London for their sustained commitment to the lives and concerns of LGBT people at SU. Their critical engagement with LGBT issues continues to both encourage and challenge SU's community—students, faculty, staff, and administrators—to make the lives of LGBT people central to the goals of the university. In addition, we are grateful to Derina Samuel and Stacey Lane Tice for providing their support, advice, and the professional opportunity to make this volume a reality.

We also appreciate the generous contribution of time, experiences, and ideas offered by the faculty and instructors who agreed to be interviewed for Part Two of this volume. This includes: Linda Alcoff (Philosophy), Barbara Applebaum (Cultural Foundations of Education), Sari Biklen (Cultural Foundations of Education), Linda Carty (African American Studies), Marj DeVault (Sociology), Lauren Eastwood (Sociology), Beth Ferri (Teaching and Leadership and Cultural Foundations of Education), Winston Grady-Willis (African American Studies), Karen Hall (English Textual Studies), Margaret Himley (Writing Program), Adrea Jaehnig (Higher Education), Kim Jaffee (Social Work), Tom Keck (Political Science), Claudia Klaver (English Textual Studies), Andrew London (Sociology), Vivian May (Women's Studies), Jackie Orr (Sociology), and Charles Sprock (Law School).

In addition, the editors would like to acknowledge the support for this volume from the Senate Committee on LGBT Concerns and the LGBT Resource Center. The Professional Development Programs of the Graduate School provided significant support and funding for the overall project and the Divisions of Undergraduate Studies and Student Affairs provided partial financial support for the printing of this volume in order to enhance, broaden, and support the academic and social experience of Syracuse University students.

Special thanks to Andrew Augeri for his creative genius in designing the cover and page layout, as well as for his patience with our often chaotic editorial process. Also, special thanks to Tina Mishko for her administrative support and excellent organizational skills.

This book is the product of a collaborative effort by over 30 volunteers. We would like to express our deep appreciation to the following contributors who volunteered their time, energy, expertise, and enthusiasm to help make this project a substantial contribution to the Syracuse University teaching community: Susan Adams, Ahoura Afshar, Dean Allbritton, Katrina Arndt, Camille Baker, Payal Banerjee, Eldar Beiseitov, Jeremy Brunson, Rachel Burgess, Paul Butler, Kelly Concannon, Melissa Conroy, Nicole Dimetman, Tom Dunn, Deborah Freund, Cyril Ghosh, Sidney Greenblatt, Patricia Hayes, Gerry Lambert, Huei-Hsuan Lin, Aman Luthra, Jonathan Massey, Rachel Moran, Adina Mulliken, Rob Pusch, Kristenne Robison, Elizabeth Sierra-Zarella, Brian Stout, Justin Welch, and Jennifer Wingard.

>>preface

Diversity at Syracuse:
An Open-ended Commitment

S yracuse University is a microcosm of today's world, enrolling representatives of most races and ethnic groups found in the United States and more than 2,000 international students from 100 countries. This is not by chance.

The University embraces diversity as one of its core values and enjoys a reputation for being an institution where disparate groups among its students, faculty, and staff come together as one community of scholars to learn from each other and to prepare for a world that every day grows increasingly more intricate and interconnected.

Diversity has been a part of the University's fiber from its very beginning. Syracuse educated the first African American woman to become a physician, never had quotas for Catholics or Jews when that was a common practice, and admitted Japanese-American students during World War II. Our commitment to diversity is, in part, a matter of upholding that tradition.

Diversity at Syracuse, however, goes beyond tradition. Cultural, ethnic, intellectual, and racial diversity has been adopted as pedagogical policy because of the richness such diversity brings to the educational environment. Academic research on the subject has been indisputably clear: Diversity within a campus community has far-ranging and significant educational benefits for everyone. As the world becomes more culturally and ethnically heterogeneous, the lessons of diversity grow increasingly relevant, helping students develop and appreciate a variety of cultural and intellectual perspectives. Students in diverse learning environments learn more, have higher levels of satisfaction, and tend to become more engaged in community life both on and off campus.

For the most part, discussion about diversity at SU has centered on issues of race and ethnicity. Now, the Graduate School, in association with the University

Senate Committee on LGBT issues and the LGBT Resource Center, is proactively extending that discussion to include diversity of sexual and gender identity.

Only recently has social discourse opened itself to frank discussion on the subject of sexual and gender identity and the issues facing those who do not conform to traditionally recognized cultural norms. The term *heteronormativity*, which you will encounter repeatedly as you use this guide, describes an ideology based on definitions of what it means to be a woman or a man that exclude and discriminate against a significant minority population. Society as a whole must come to terms with heteronormativity and related social and cultural issues. However, as a leading academic institution—and in particular one that has been at the vanguard of social justice—it is incumbent on us to engage these issues, introduce them into our classroom discussions and lead the way to a more harmonious society based on acceptance, understanding, and inclusion.

An integral part of the Syracuse experience and a cornerstone of the Academic Plan, diversity expands and redefines knowledge within the academy as it prepares our graduates for success in an increasingly diverse and interdependent world. Whether that preparation involves developing and appreciating a variety of intellectual perspectives, acquiring personal skills in order to manage future social and civic responsibilities, or refining professional tools to put to work in pursuing one's career, diversity is an ever-present imperative. As members of the Syracuse University teaching community, I encourage you to embrace the goals of diversity wholeheartedly—a good place to start is by absorbing the lessons in this resource guide. Only by working together in this cause will Syracuse remain a place where diversity flourishes and where all people are accepted and respected.

Deborah A. Freund

Deborah A. Freund
Vice Chancellor and Provost
Professor of Public Administration

Introduction:
Interrupting Expectations

Mary Queen, Kathleen Farrell, and Nisha Gupta

This book is not a "how-to" manual on LGBT pedagogy. It will not give you specific assignments to use in your classrooms, nor will it provide you with "scripts" to use when talking with students about LGBT issues. Why have you been asked to read this book, then? The three brief comments below, from undergraduate students here at Syracuse University, capture the essence of an "issue," and the teaching practices that reinforce it, that we problematize in this volume. Take a look at this:

> I took French classes last year, and even though my TA seemed very liberal, as part of getting us to speak in French, she'd ask questions like "How would you describe your ideal boyfriend?" and "How would you describe your future plans for marriage and children?" I know it was unintentional, but it felt like my whole existence was erased.

And this:

> I was just in a class that covers progressive issues and we were talking about how gay people are oppressed. It was nice that nobody really said anything derogatory towards LGBT people, but all of the other guys felt compelled to keep saying things like, "I'm straight," and "but I'm not gay" while talking about these issues. I was almost tempted to make up a girlfriend or something just so everyone wouldn't know I was gay. It was almost like I had to match up to their masculinity. I really felt like I wasn't good enough to give my opinions because I wasn't straight.

And this:

> It sucks how the entire burden of making the classroom a safe space can fall on the shoulders of queer students. I would think that a classroom that feels like a safe space would be a more comfortable environment for everybody. I don't know whether my TAs and professors are scared of dealing with this stuff or if they just have the privilege of not thinking about it.

These students, from a range of academic disciplines, may be in your class this semester. How will you create an environment that acknowledges and respects their experiences and concerns? Here's something more to consider: despite recent efforts by administrators, staff, students, and faculty here at SU, a particular ideology, responsible for these students' discomfort, continues to impair our learning and living environments because it often masquerades as something else, thus hiding the way it actually operates. What is this system of beliefs? Did you guess *homophobia*? Homophobia—languages and practices that support discrimination against and fear/hatred of LGBT people—is indeed one part of this pervasive problem. Homophobia, however, is merely the mask through which we glimpse aspects of a larger systemic concern: *heteronormativity*. Efforts to eradicate homophobia largely fail because, as SU faculty Barbara Applebaum points out, "You cannot understand homophobia without understanding heteronormativity."

"Interrupting Heteronormativity" is grounded in two assumptions: first, that as a teaching assistant, you care about the work you do as an educator; and second, that as an employee of Syracuse University, you accept your responsibility to work toward fulfilling the mission of the university. A central focus of this mission, as Vice-Chancellor Deborah Freund points out in the "Preface" to this volume, is to provide students with an environment rich in diversity in order to prepare them for living and working in a heterogeneous world. For Syracuse University, this conception of diversity includes *sexual* and *gender diversity*. Freund writes: "as a leading academic institution—and in particular one that has been at the vanguard of social justice—it is incumbent on us to engage these issues [of heteronormativity], introduce them into our classroom discussions and lead the way to a more harmonious society based on acceptance, understanding, and inclusion" (Preface). As a responsible employee of SU, and as a response-able teacher, it is essential that you understand, acknowledge, and consistently work to interrupt heteronormative classroom practices that silence many students and inhibit the learning processes of everyone on this campus.

Although the term "heteronormativity" is gaining some currency in pedagogical theories and practices, the term is often left out of discussions about "diversity" altogether. Heteronormativity sounds complex, but is actually quite simple. As a term, heteronormativity describes the processes through which social institutions and social policies reinforce the belief that human beings fall into two distinct sex/gender categories: male/man and female/woman. This belief (or ideology) produces a correlative belief that those two sexes/genders exist in order to fulfill complementary roles, i.e., that all intimate relationships ought to exist only between males/men and females/women. To describe a social institution as heteronormative means that it has visible or hidden norms, some of which are viewed as normal only for males/men and others which are seen as normal only for females/women. As a concept, heteronormativity is used to help identify the processes through which individuals who do not appear to "fit" or individuals who refuse to "fit" these norms are made invisible and silenced. Heteronormative institutions and practices, then, block access to full legal, political, economic, educational, and social participation for millions of individuals in the U.S. This anti-democratic, exclusionary ideology undermines the fundamental mission of Syracuse University.

Our purpose in this book is twofold: first, to make visible the everyday, seemingly inconsequential ways in which our classrooms become sites for the reinforcement of heteronormative ideologies and practices that inhibit student learning as well as student-teacher and student-student interactions. And second, to help you learn how to identify, bring attention to, and work with your students to *interrupt* these ideologies and practices in your classroom. In addition to its focus on "practical" classroom concerns, this book also provides a conceptual framework or *pedagogy*—an approach to or perspective on teaching—for thinking about but also beyond the course content, to include students' relation to the material, the experiences and knowledge students bring into the classroom, the particular classroom structures, course units, or sequences and their relation to the goals of the course, your role in students' learning processes, peers' roles in students' learning, students' roles in your teaching, the examples you use, the technology you use, and so on. In essence, your *pedagogy* provides the reasons for why you do what you do in the classroom. The *LGBT pedagogy* in this book provides you with an approach to teaching that foregrounds the ways in which heteronormative ideologies and practices are embedded in all classrooms, and suggests ways to interrupt those practices in order to create the most effective learning environment for all students in your classroom. In a very real sense, then, the *LGBT pedagogy* in this book challenges you to work toward fulfilling the educational mission of this institution, rather than simply fulfilling particular course or disciplinary goals. One of our fundamental responsibilities as teachers at SU is to engage with students in a collaborative effort to examine and interrupt the limits of our experiences, perspectives, and knowledges in order to create spaces for a socially-just vision of the world.

This book had its genesis in the work of the University Senate Committee on LGBT Concerns. Through a 2003 Vision Fund Grant, the committee began a "self-study" of the needs and interests of students, interest and expertise of faculty, and current course offerings in order to evaluate how and where LGBT issues might enter into the curriculum and SU community. As part of efforts to disseminate their findings and ideas, co-chairs Margaret Himley and Andrew London presented on LGBT Pedagogy at the Future Professoriate Program's Minnowbrook conference in May of 2003. Stacey Lane Tice, Assistant Dean of the Graduate School and Director of the TA Program, coordinated that presentation, and then in conversation with Himley and London, developed the idea to produce a book on LGBT pedagogy for incoming graduate teaching assistants in the fall of 2004. From this conversation, Stacey Lane Tice, Margaret Himley, Andrew London, Adrea Jaehnig (Director of the LGBT Resource Center), and Derina Samuel (Associate Director for Professional Development Programs of the Graduate School) formed an editorial board and invited us—graduate students Kathleen

4

Farrell (Sociology), Mary Queen (The Writing Program), and Nisha Gupta (Cultural Foundations of Education)—to serve as editors.

During our initial editorial meetings, we made the decision to first create the framework and contents for the book, and then send out a campus-wide call for volunteers who would contribute in various ways: as essayists, interviewers, interviewees, researchers, and designers. We also invited graduate students whose work we knew focused on issues of race, ethnicity, socioeconomics, (dis)ability, gender, and nationality to contribute their disciplinary expertise to this volume. We sought undergraduate students whose ideas and experiences could provide concrete evidence for the importance, even necessity, of identifying the heteronormative practices in classroom interactions, assignments, and examples, and working to interrupt those practices through LGBT pedagogical frameworks. And, we invited a cadre of faculty across disciplines to discuss their "LGBT-supportive" pedagogical ideas and teaching experiences with graduate student interviewers.

Finally, throughout our "recruiting" process, we emphasized the necessity for a range of perspectives and identities. We identified very early on that this book, while focused on LGBT pedagogy, could not ignore the fundamental connections among LGBT concerns and issues and those of other communities on campus who struggle for visibility and voice: people with disabilities, people of color, and feminists, among others. Also, in order to demonstrate to you that a *LGBT pedagogy* in your classroom practices is not only possible, but important and desirable for all teachers, including those who do not identify as LGBT, we have included the experiences, ideas, and voices of individuals who do not identify as LGBT. The efforts of straight (or heterosexual) allies to make SU more visibly- and structurally-supportive of the LGBT community has been and continues to be essential to the success of SU's LGBT community. This book reflects their efforts, as well as the efforts of LGBT-identified people.

Our initial conception of the framework for this volume has, surprisingly, remained consistent throughout the year-long process. The book is divided into three parts: Part One is comprised of ten essays that discuss various aspects of and perspectives on heteronormativity. These ten essays are grouped into subsections: the first section, "Framing the Issues," does just that. In the first essay, "Heteronormativity and Teaching at Syracuse University," Susan Adams examines the pervasiveness and invisibility of heteronormativity in our culture through her discussion of concrete examples—from pop culture and from the scientific community—and demonstrates the effects of this on classroom practices. In "Cartography of (Un)Intelligibility: A Migrant Intellectual's Tale of the Field," Huei Lin reflects on the implications of students' expectations of teacher-training and "diversity pedagogy," as well as the challenges to her "interruption" of those expectations. Ahoura Afshar, in "The Invisible Presence of Sexuality in the Classroom," argues for the importance of acknowledging the ways in which ideas about and expressions of sexuality are always embedded in classroom lessons and interactions.

The second section, "Listening to Students," gives you perspectives from graduate and undergraduate students at SU. In the first essay of this section, "(Un)straightening the SU Landscape" Aman Luthra—a recent graduate from the Geography department—shows us how heteronormativity intersects with the physical landscape of the SU campus. Undergraduates Brian Stout and Rachel Moran collaborated to give us an unsettling but important account of their experiences with homophobic behavior and heteronormative ideologies and practices both in and outside of the classroom spaces at SU in their essay, "Echoes of Silence: Experiences of LGBT College Students at SU." Another undergraduate, Camille Baker, follows up with an essay describing "The Importance of LGBT Allies" at SU. The final essay in this second section, a collaborative essay by graduate students Eldar Beiseitov and Payal Banerjee, describes "Queer TA's in the Classroom: Perspectives on Coming Out."

The third section of Part One, "Engaging Nuances," delineates some of the depth and nuance to the issues presented in this volume. Nicole Dimetman surveys our cultural landscape in "Understanding Current LGBT-Related Policies and Debates" and provides a thoughtful and thorough explanation of the current status of LGBT concerns in the U.S. In "(Trans)Gendering the Classroom," Rob Pusch challenges us to think beyond gender binaries to the experiences of transgender students in our very gender-normed classrooms. The final essay, Sidney Greenblatt's "International Students and Sexuality at Syracuse University," moves outward to focus on international students' encounters with heteronormative practices and LGBT identities on SU's campus. This piece foregrounds the importance of understanding how the intersections of cultural, national, geopolitical, and religious identities affect students' and our own relation to "diversity."

The second part of the book, "Responsible Teaching," is a celebration of the best LGBT pedagogical practices of various SU faculty members. Rather than create an instructional manual on how to "do" LGBT pedagogy, we opted to ask our seasoned faculty how they do it. Almost a dozen interviewers set out across campus to talk with almost two dozen teachers and the resulting hundreds of pages of transcripts were edited down to one essay by Elizabeth Sierra-Zarella, a graduate student in Child and Family Studies. "Constant Queerying: Practicing Responsible Pedagogy at Syracuse University," plays with the interaction between "query" (question) and "queer" to create a rich "conversation" that highlights faculty's successes, their struggles, and their understanding of the work to be done. This essay is followed by a related conversation, "Toward a LGBT Studies Minor," in which members of the Senate Committee on LGBT Concerns discuss the challenges of creating a LGBT minor that could provide a space in the curriculum devoted to sustained inquiry into theories, histories, literature, and activist movements that have formed a politics of identity called LGBT.

"Interrupting Heteronormativity" was designed as a teaching resource guide; we see each essay in this volume as a pedagogical resource meant to inform your teaching practices around heteronormativity. However, we also know that this book is incomplete; many readers may find that its goals require additional work beyond these pages. The third part of this volume, "LGBT Teaching Resources" was designed as a starting point for those instructors who want to learn more about the LGBT community, LGBT pedagogy, and academic work on these areas. Within this section you will find Dean Allbritton's, "Using Film Inclusively: Or, Queering Your Classroom," a valuable contribution focusing movies with LGBT content and the possible uses of these in a wide range of academic courses. Following this, we've included local Syracuse and Syracuse University LGBT community resources, including political, social, and religious groups, businesses, and meeting spots, compiled by undergraduate Justin Welch. Our list of Online LGBT Resources will introduce you to many national groups as well as help you find LGBT facts and statistics. Reference Librarian Adina Mulliken assembled an abundant list of academic texts that address various aspects of LGBT pedagogy and campus life and her bibliography is included here, followed by a more general list of academic sources addressing sexuality and gender studies. Our resource section ends with a LGBT glossary of terms, to help you maneuver your way through this new world of ideas and terms.

When the editors asked Patty Hayes (Graduate Assistant at the LGBT Resource Center) to write a short reflection on the post-production session for the student writers/ editors and faculty advisors of the *Student Voice* special issue on SU's LGBT community (May 6-12, 2004), she responded with a reflection that concludes with this comment:

As I sat and listened to the students, one after the other, talk about their own personal epiphanies, I marveled at their courage and honesty. Certainly, what started out for some "merely" as a class project, was a catalyst of sorts, both personally and professionally. Clearly, the learning that took place in the course of this assignment went well beyond what any syllabus or course description could predict. What more could one ask for in terms of getting an education?

To us, this exemplifies the kind of learning that can happen when students, staff, administrators, and faculty demand experiences that stretch us beyond our "comfort zones" to encounter and interact with others on their terms. Clearly, the students in these Newhouse classes (assigned to produce this special issue) learned about the LGBT community not by demanding that this community explain itself to them, but rather, by listening closely, listening respectfully, and listening responsibly as this community shared with the students what it means to live as LGBT in a world structured by heteronormativity. We hope that you, too, will listen closely, respectfully, and responsibly to the ideas and experiences of students, staff, and faculty presented in this book. This volume is an opportunity for you to challenge and transform your own pedagogical beliefs and practices.

>>We thank Patty Hayes for providing her reflections on the post-production discussions of the *Student Voice* special issue on the LGBT community at SU.

Interrupting
Heteronormativity

PART I

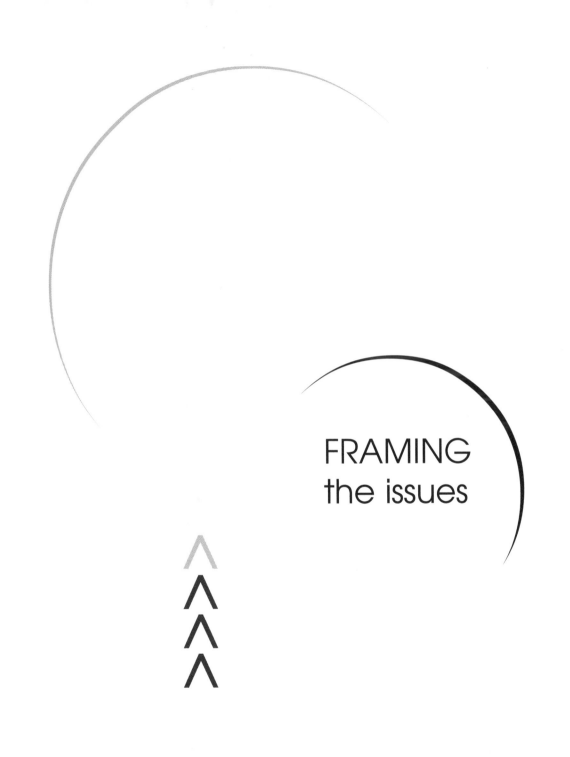

FRAMING
the issues

Heteronormativity and Teaching at Syracuse University

Susan Adams

Man, I Feel Uncomfortable

A recent television commercial shows five men in a Chevy Colorado pickup truck, the radio blasting Shania Twain's "Man! I Feel Like a Woman." One man, seated in the center of the back seat of the crew cab, is singing happily along: "The best thing about being a woman / Is the prerogative to have a little fun!" The others wear uncomfortable expressions on their faces, particularly those on either side of the singer; the camera focuses on a knee shifted away, demonstrating the roominess of the truck's back seat.[1]

Discomfort, of course, is the source of much contemporary humor, which often stems from dissonance or friction between what we expect and what actually occurs. On *Friends*, for example, we laugh when Phoebe's song about animals in the barnyard becomes an exposé of the meat industry—we don't *expect* people to sing about such things to small children. The raw humor of the Farrelly Brothers' movies and the droll wit of Ellen DeGeneres's standup comedy operate in similar ways,

disrupting audience expectations.

We *expect* a truckload of guys racing across a desert landscape to be macho men, ogling rather than empathizing with women. Such expectations constitute our sense of normalcy, the regular day-to-day operations of our world. The "normal" being disrupted in the Chevy commercial is the normal of gender boundaries and this causes discomfort for the other passengers. We might call this homophobia, echoing the sentiments of *AdAge.com* columnist Bob Garfield (2004) who calls the commercial "kinda cute and kinda homophobic." This concept, however, fails to fully account for the range of gender and sexual expectations at work here.

What's expected here is heterosexuality. Two genders, each sexually attracted to the other. Clear boundaries. No exceptions. The discomfort evidenced by the four non-singing men results not (merely) from a fear of homosexual advances by the Twain fan. This commercial, part of Chevrolet's "American Revolution" campaign, demonstrates the deeply institutionalized

nature of our binary gender system. Gender is certainly *not* included in this revolution. How far does this institutionalization extend? What questions do we need to ask of the world around us to begin to disturb the taken-for-granted nature of gender and sexuality? What critical concepts can make this work possible?

Compulsory Heterosexuality and Heteronormativity

Those of us asking such questions experience our own sense of dis-ease in the world. We might find the costuming of gender an uncomfortable fit; sexual attraction may not follow societal dictates. Adrienne Rich's (1980) influential essay "Compulsory Heterosexuality and Lesbian Existence" argues that heterosexuality is taken as a given, as the natural order of things, effectively erasing (or at minimum, marginalizing) lesbian experience. In response, Rich coined the term "compulsory heterosexuality" to describe the unquestioned status of this particular ordering of the world, further noting "the economic imperative to heterosexuality and marriage and to the sanctions imposed against single women and widows […]" (p. 634). Rich argues for the analysis of heterosexuality as a political institution (p. 637).

Queer theorists extend this idea, placing the entire matrix of gender and sexuality on the table. Gender, that sense of belonging to a particular category of persons (usually "male" or "female"), is intricately wound up in sexuality, often understood to mean "whom do you desire."[2] Within contemporary Western culture's binary gender system, one is expected to desire—to love—someone of the opposite gender. Michael Warner (2002) employs the term "heteronormativity" to more effectively probe the "complex cluster of sexual practices [that] gets confused, in heterosexual culture, with the love plot of intimacy and familialism that signifies belonging to society in a deep and normal way" (p. 194). Warner continues:

> A whole field of social relations becomes intelligible as heterosexuality, and this privatized sexual culture bestows on its sexual practices a tacit sense of rightness and normalcy. This sense of rightness—embedded in things and not just in sex—is what we call heteronormativity (p. 194).

This sense of rightness is very strong. Even those of us who experience discrimination based on sexual orientation easily overlook the simple, everyday ways

that normative gender and sexuality are reinforced. For example, a lesbian friend expressed her discomfort with transgendered individuals who pursue surgical options. When I suggested, following scholars such as Anne Fausto-Sterling (2000), that gender is more of a continuum or statistical distribution, she balked: "There are two bathroom doors—men's and women's—and that's it." Clearly the implication is that any "choice" has been made for us by "nature," and it's our job as individuals to learn to accept, and fit in to, these two "choices."

But is it really that clear or simple? Bathrooms offer an excellent example of the challenge of such choices. Women, who, like my friend, are more comfortable in pants, or women who walk with confidence and wear short hair, or women

HETERONORMATIVITY
pervades
EVERY
aspect of
<our>
lives and work...

15

who exhibit "male" characteristics such as facial hair, find themselves policed by others. "This is the *ladies'* room," they're told. The rebuke may be an honest mistake (we are taught to read gender quickly), or it may be a hostile attack. Honest mistakes—such as when a rushed clerk calls me "sir"—cause tremendous embarrassment to the individual making the error. While we might hope that such mistakes would open up discussion about the fluidity of gender, those making the errors are usually too embarrassed or angry for that to happen. Rob S. Pusch discusses this phenomenon more fully in his essay in this volume, "(Trans)Gendering the Classroom," noting that blame is usually assigned to the person who could not be quickly identified as male or female. Such blame can be accompanied by life-threatening violence—the boundaries are aggressively policed.

Gender and sexual object choice are, then, deeply ingrained in all of us—even when we may think of ourselves (not without justification) as well educated in these issues. Heteronormativity is reified— "embedded in things," as Warner observed—in ordinary, everyday activities: wedding magazines with spectacular brides on the covers; men's magazines that usually feature scantily dressed women; toy store aisles divided into pink and black; bathroom doors marked "Men" and "Women." To "feel like a woman" (to quote Shania) is, as Judith Butler (1990) asserted, "an effect and function of a decidedly public and social discourse, the public regulation of fantasy through the surface politics of the body [...]" (p. 136). To feel like a man, as evidenced by the four uncomfortable inhabitants of the pickup truck, is no less policed by the gender border patrol.

Great, But What Does This Have To Do With What I Teach?

What Warner makes clear in his discussion of heteronormativity is its insidious and invasive nature: heteronormativity pervades every aspect of our lives and work. From framing research questions to evaluating the credibility of sources, the unquestioned assumptions of gender and sexuality structure our thinking, limiting the scope of possibility. Our jobs as scholars and teachers often require us to push ourselves and our students to ask the difficult questions, to step out of our respective comfort zones and peel up the edges of apparent certainties.

But such destabilization can be painful—even for those of us who don't feel at ease with gender norms. For those students who face material risks—whose religious or family convictions explicitly and rigidly affirm specific heteronorms— questioning assumptions must be undertaken with care and sensitivity. It must be remembered that heteronormativity operates within a matrix of other cultural norms: race, ethnicity, (dis)ability, age, religion, and so forth. Each of these brings its own complexities and challenges.

And yet, opening up inquiry is essential to higher education. How can we assist students in developing newer, more significant investigations when some of the most fundamental aspects of all of our lives go unquestioned? First, we can recognize our own complicity in heteronormative systems. Several writers in this volume describe circumstances in which instructors failed to recognize the ways in which their own behaviors—reactions to a name, for instance (see Pusch), or assuming a student was straight (see Stout and Moran)—reinforced those systems. Stout and Moran also describe an instructor using overtly heterosexual exercises in a foreign language class—a situation easily avoided through awareness and advance preparation.

Instructors in the sciences may not immediately see the relevance of this to their own teaching. I offer the following example as a reminder of the role language plays in constructing (and restricting) understanding in all our fields. Earlier this year, scientists from Harvard Medical School and the Massachusetts General Hospital published findings in the journal

VOICES

You cannot understand homophobia without understanding heteronormativity.

>Barbara Applebaum (Cultural Foundations of Education)

Nature with the potential to disrupt our understanding of reproduction. The accepted "dogma" that female mammals are born with a finite number of eggs (while males continue to produce sperm throughout their lives), according to these researchers, may not be true (Johnson et al., 2004).

Of course, all fields make discoveries, or approach issues from new perspectives, or introduce new theories. What makes this discovery of interest is why the "dogma" remained unquestioned. Emily Martin argues in her 1991 article "The Egg and the Sperm" that researchers perpetuate heteronormative readings of sexual reproduction by relying on gendered stereotypes. The view that eggs—or more accurately, ovarian follicles containing ova—are present at birth coincides nicely with a view of females as passive and receptive. As Martin observes, scientific articles and textbooks contrast male enthusiasm with female passivity: "Far from being *produced*, as sperm are, they [ova] merely sit on the shelf, slowly degenerating and aging like overstocked inventory" (p. 487). Science actually constructs a fairy tale romance for egg and sperm, describing how the egg is "swept" along the fallopian tube, while those enthusiastic sperm "propel" and "penetrate" (Martin, 2004, p. 489). The findings of Johnson and his colleagues demonstrate that norms perpetuate gender expectations and assumptions that might not actually be true.

expressions

HETEROSEXISM

>>>the dominant cultural belief that heterosexuality is the one "normal" and "right" sexuality for all people

That spirit of inquiry that brings us to scholarship and teaching can be easily stifled by textbooks—and instructors—who fail to question assumptions. The discourses of heteronormativity that pervade our lives and studies need to be challenged continually. Dr. Allan Spradling responded to the Harvard study in a report on National Public Radio's Morning Edition. As reporter Jon Hamilton noted, Spradling "studies fruit flies and notes that the females continue to produce new eggs throughout their lives. But until he heard about [this] study, he'd simply accepted that mammals weren't like fruit flies." Hamilton declared, "My personal reaction when I heard it was, you know, I never should have believed that. You know, why wasn't I more skeptical?" (NPR, 2004).

>>REFERENCES

Butler, J. (1990). *Gender trouble: Feminism and the subversion of identity.* New York: Routledge.

Fausto-Sterling, A. (2000). *Sexing the body: Gender politics and the construction of sexuality.* New York: Basic Books.

Garfield, B. (2004). Swearing at America's revolution. *AdAge.* Retrieved January 16, 2004, from http://www.adage.com.

Johnson, J., Canning, J., Kaneko, T., Pru, J., & Tilly, J. (2004). Germline stem cells and follicular renewal in the postnatal mammalian ovary. *Nature, 428* (March 11), 145-150.

Martin, E. (1991). The egg and the sperm: How science has constructed a romance based on stereotypical male-female roles. *Signs: Journal of Women in Culture and Society*, 16 (3), 485-501.

National Public Radio. (2004, March 11). New research finds possible hope for middle-aged women to have babies. *Morning edition.* (Available from National Public Radio, 635 Massachusetts Ave., NW, Washington, D.C. 20001)

Piligan, E. A new campaign from Chevrolet. Retrieved January 16, 2004 from http://www.michaelbay.com

Rich, Adrienne. (1980). Compulsory heterosexuality and lesbian experience. *Signs: Journal of Women in Culture and Society,* 5, 631-660.

Warner, M. (2000). *The trouble with normal: Sex, politics, and the ethics of queer life.* Cambridge: Harvard University Press.

Warner, M. (2002). *Publics and counterpublics.* New York: Zone.

>>ENDNOTES

1 > While Chevrolet does not include this among the commercials to be viewed on its website, it is receiving regular airplay. In addition, interested readers can access filmmaker Michael Bay's description of the spot at www.michaelbay.com (Pilligan, 2003).

2 > For a fuller definition of the term "gender," see Pusch's essay in this volume.

Cartography of (Un)Intelligibility:
A Migrant Intellectual's Tale of the Field

Huei-Hsuan Lin

"I am not a confused person" (Mohanty 2003). Articulating a location for myself, nevertheless, is always a mind-boggling task that I undertake reluctantly. To name myself as a "migrant intellectual" in this essay does not mean that there is an "authentically" migrant perspective and I make a perfect fit to its taxonomy. Rather, enunciating a location for myself is a deliberate act to initiate a process through which I examine my relationship to others in the geo-political, cultural and educational landscape of which I am a part.

Madan Sarup (1994) defines a migrant as "a person who has crossed the border. S/he seeks a place to make 'a new beginning,' to start again, to make a better life" (p. 94). The migrant, encountering both hostility and welcome, inclusion and exclusion, becomes a stranger as well as a historical and social actor in a forever strange, yet increasingly familiar land.

Like many of the "international" graduate students in America, I came to the States for advanced degrees after completing my undergraduate education in my home country, Taiwan. I currently teach in Syracuse University at the department of Cultural Foundations of Education (CFE), from which I received my doctoral degree. CFE is an interdisciplinary department, which aims to examine the power relations embedded within the social institution of education. It encourages scholarships and pedagogies that explore the politics of knowledge through interrogating how educational practices, policies, and schooling experiences are constructed. Cultural Foundations, as a discipline, validates my pursuit of liberation as an intellectual mission, provides me with languages to name privilege and oppression, and guides me to make sense of, unlearn, and negotiate with, my upbringing. In many ways I do consider myself a "home-grown" Ph. D. in this teaching and research institution, but only to find out that I'm "always-already an outsider within" (Cervenak, et al., 2002, p. 342).

That is, my training in and appointment with this American institution of higher learning which prioritizes the promotion of "diversity" as one of its utmost official agendas, allows me to fashion intellectual, ideological, social, cultural, and emotional ties with the status quo who hires me, with my colleagues and friends with whom I work and learn, and with students who I interact with and deeply care about. While this "insider relationship" is fulfilling and gratifying, my location as an exploited intellectual migrant worker in the political economy, and the fixation of the ascribed meanings attached to my visible and audible identity constantly remind me of the "strangeness" that my presence embodies and my position comprises. Patricia Hill Collins (1990) coins this "curious outsider-within stance" and articulates the epistemological and political potential of this peculiar marginality that can stimulate a "distinctive angle of vision" on social relations and institutional policies and practices. It is from this precarious location of an outsider within and insider without that I approach education with a social justice agenda as a discursive site

Conversely, part of being **privileged** is that you do have the **luxury** of just "being"

and the <**credibility**> is granted to **you** by default.

22

marked by social and epistemological differentiation and openness to otherness and change.

I have witnessed teaching assistants from my department, both International and American-born, struggle in their teaching debut in American higher education. I do believe there is always room for improvement in our teaching, and the point of consideration involves how we should proceed with discussion of pedagogy in ways that challenge "habits of being" so that pedagogical deliberation enriches our personal and intellectual growth as well as shakes up the institution culturally and politically. As situated within a larger, on-going reflexive project on diversity pedagogy, this essay presumes that the TAs' (in my department as well as those beyond) linguistic, conceptual, cultural, and psychological struggles can contribute to the making of collective pedagogical/institutional memories and texts that open up opportunities to deconstruct the engrained ways of looking and evaluating. Assuming "migrant intellectual" as "a location of critical practice" that enables specific modes of reading and knowing in American academia, this paper aims to demonstrate a way of thinking through what teaching from the location of a female migrant scholar offers to the re/thinking of liberatory education and the politics of

knowledge. To do so, I will unravel the complex entanglements underlying the social and educational spaces in which I interact with the institution and with my undergraduate students, who appear to be predominantly white, heterosexual, and from upper and middle class families from the northeast U.S.

In this essay, I employ the framework of "geographical imaginations" using theories of location, borders, and movement that seek to change power relations within educational spaces. Additionally, I foreground classroom relations and draw on queer pedagogy to trouble assumptions pertaining to appropriateness, legitimacy, and comprehensibility. Queer pedagogy, according to Deborah Britzman (1995), identifies two sets of questions essential to my investigation of "diversity pedagogy" that problematize "the conceptual geography of normalization" (p. 2). According to Britzman, any educational commitment to social equity has to engage "questions concerning what education, knowledge, and identity have to do with fashioning structures of thinkability and the limits of thought" (p. 13). In addition to analyzing education as a normalization process that refuses and/or appropriates "differences," Queer Theory commits us to another, interrelated set of questions "concerning what education has to do with the possibilities of proliferating identifications and critiques that exceed identity, yet still hold onto the understanding of identity as a state of emergency" (p. 13). In other words, Britzman cautions us about the inclination of pigeonholing the significance of social experiences into rigidly prescribed social categories, as she encourages us to consider education a paradoxical space where both oblivion and renunciation as well as imagination and acknowledgement of differences can occur.

In what follows I look at two related pedagogical moments to think through the relationship between social locations and habits and ways of thinking in concrete educational encounters. Through these accounts I intend to obscure the tendency in current diversity discourse that regards "alternative knowledge" simply as historical and lived experiences, "heritages," and stories told by the "marginal" groups. This approach intends to "make room" to accommodate voices of the under-represented groups, but falls short of interrogating how the dominant culture structures and regulates different ways of thinking and relating to the world in ways that naturalize the unequal social arrangement. In doing so, this popular practice of diversity pedagogy, intended to compensate those who have been previously denied visibility, protects the hegemony of dominant power, rather than produces and encourages critical perspectives and alternative accounts.

Though in crafting this essay I pay special attention not to distance myself from the material lives of American higher education students, I am acutely cognizant of the possible reading that constructs my teaching as a terrain of antagonism, positioning foreign-born instructors in opposition to predominantly American white undergraduates. Thus I invite you, in addition to seeing the educational locale discussed in this tale as a space of tension, to recognize it as a field that houses new subjects of criticism. That is, interpreting teaching from the location of migrant intellectual in the American educational context enables us to critically examine the relationship between (un) intelligibility [i.e., what is (in) comprehensible], social location, and the transnational politics of knowledge production. This account, examining the inscriptions that legitimate and inhibit pedagogical practices, is intended to push "diversity pedagogy" to address what is dismissed or cannot bear to be known in normative educational encounters.

I teach a course in which I invite pre-service teachers to grapple with the idea that teachers are "public intellectuals" whose work defines, concerns, and shapes public issues. Teaching, like any social endeavor, is a practice situated within its immediate and larger academic context. The first three semesters I taught this course, I received polite inquiries from students wondering why I didn't ask them to do the traditional project of creating a blueprint for "multicultural schools." This question reflected what they learned from those who previously took this course as a "good" practice that needed to be kept since students (about 90% of whom are white) were asked to interview their peers on campus who were from backgrounds different from their own (usually that meant students of color and occasionally students with disabilities and LGBT students). In this project students incorporated the information they collected from interviews into their work of imagining new multicultural schools. For me, students without additional training in data analysis tended to take the comments they gathered at face value and rendered this assignment a "rainbow ensemble." That is, these projects collected and presented "opinions" and "voices" as a "harmonious ensemble," devoid of contested social, historical, and political inequalities and normative ideologies. Projects like these also tended to pride themselves for "objectively" portraying various groups' schooling experiences, as if they were transparent and equally positioned.

Having said that, my take on the assignment is not at issue here, rather it is that the students did not construct their inquiries as opportunities to engage in deliberation about diversity pedagogy with me. The students who approached me seemed attuned to the institutionally sanctioned power dynamic between teachers and students, i.e. they were courteous and diplomatic in questioning my pedagogy. Nonetheless, they failed to recognize that they already measured the way I, a foreign-accented/looking female instructor, teach the course against the claimed tradition created by a white, male, seasoned colleague. Their inquiries provide

25

evidence regarding how the hegemony of convention and the production of normalcy operate. That is, "what it has been" is conflated with "what it should be" unless there is a good explanation. Inquiries like this placed the responsibility on those whose thinking and bodies are marked as strangers to work harder to gain and prove their legitimacy. Conversely, part of being privileged is that you do have the luxury of just "being" and the credibility is granted to you by default. You don't have to be defined, but get to define the "otherness" of the "other."

A white male graduate student from the College of Arts and Sciences was concerned with my interpretation of student encounters like this. With apprehension, he asked, "How do you know what you know is right? Why couldn't it just be considered an innocent inquiry about the rationales of two different assignments?" He raised the response that many of us come upon often and find ourselves defenseless against since we cannot "scientifically" defend our impressions of students' responses. His question itself, however, alludes to the production of normalcy, ignorance, and knowledge—why is interpreting from the language of individual curiosity welcomed, while normalization as an interpretive framework feels far less comforting and easily gets avoided and dismissed? Neither he nor I

entered into this interpretive situation devoid of presumptions and stances. The way I made sense of the inquiry, nonetheless, was immediately read off as a view imbued with self-interest, bias, and subjectivities. He insisted on psychologizing the interaction, which ignored the power dynamic from which an inquiry is made. Hiding itself behind the pretense of objectivity and innocence, the acclaimed view from "nowhere" continued to situate itself as the center, the norm, by refusing the alternative accounts of the shared realities to inch into their consciousness (Delpit, 1988). The issue here is not about converting views, but pedagogically how a "diversity education" can/should bring the ordinary politics of everyday interaction and teaching to the forefront of discussion so that we get to reflexively study the differing locations, frames of references, codes and interests through and with which we read and interpret the world. As we should be cautious of not positioning various interpretations only in opposition to each other, the pedagogical endeavor of constructing them "dialogically" needs to interrogate the consequences of and the extents to which different readings interrupt and/or reinscribe normative social orders, in order to facilitate conditions that "proliferate" critical accounts and practices rather than naturalizing social relations.

For years I have been striving for greater clarity and interaction to enhance the effectiveness of how I communicate my thoughts to students through the teaching format of "lectures." It is my belief that my struggling with producing "effective lectures" provides a fertile ground to excavate how normalization functions in relation to the politics of knowledge. Due to the size of my classes and other institutional constraints, lecture has been one of the few channels through which I communicate with my undergraduate students and it has become one of the most challenging aspects of teaching that demands physical, intellectual, and psychic deliberation and endurance. To start with, I am hesitant to lecture as a means of instruction. Like many "pedagogically-minded" lecturers, I learned from workshops, textbooks, and other model teachings to make the lecture space more engaging by incorporating visual aids, inviting students to participate, using topics and examples relevant to students' lives, and so on. However, lectures still remain the least satisfactory and rewarding teaching endeavor for me. Many times I have looked at my self-proclaimed "well thought-out lesson plans" and felt that a "successful" lecture was a mission impossible for me.

Confronted with the pedagogical moment of bewilderment, I resorted to feminist pedagogy literature for perspectives to make sense of this "communication" barrier. Some feminist teachers (e.g. Bell, Morrow, & Tastsoglou, 1999) explore students' resistance to courses that encourage them to interrogate the privileges they embody, while others (e.g., Cervenak et al., 2002) discuss how students construct theory in opposition to practice and resist theoretical works through silence. Certainly let's not underestimate how my public speaking skills and personae might have factored into the delivery and effectiveness of the lecture, and I realize that working on ways to improve my lecture teaching is a constant and consistent effort for professional development. While all issues aforementioned offer useful angles to look at the communicativeness of lectures, here

expressions

HEGEMONY

>>>seduces us into believing that things are the way they are because "they're supposed to be."

27

my focus is on the politics and terms of "reception."

A student wrote last year in the course evaluation, "The lectures have interesting material in them. But I feel Professor Lin tends to 'dance around' the topic. It is much clearer to the class when the idea being taught is simply and clearly stated and then elaborated on afterwards." I singled this comment out because the message is telling. For one, I optimistically read the language of "dancing around" as indicative of the possibility that the student came to see my conception of lecture and instruction as choreography or orchestration. Even if that reading might be somewhat of a stretch, this student noted that my communication style reflects a spiral and metaphorical way of thinking. This was not the first time that students have asked me to "get to the point." Very often these reminders were presented to me in the form of, what I call, "the rhetoric of confusion," i.e., "I am confused (by you)". It is important to understand the "to the point" requests intertexually. That means, coupled with comments like "Tell me what I'm supposed to get out of this," and "What do you want us to do?", some more thoughtful students would suggest ways that I could engage them better. For example, it was recommended I use bullet points to break down short narratives in handouts so that it would be easy to follow and understand.

The first time I shared this story with a group of graduate students, one white female student responded with the intention to console me, "Oh, I babble all the time." However, I do make a distinction between making a point in a circular manner from babbling (although the line is not always clear). The evaluation cited above is one of a handful of cases in which students were actually able to see the effort to make a point by covering a wider landscape. What matters here is that "a structure of intelligibility" is subtly, firmly, yet invisibly at work regulating what is and is not intelligible, even when patterns of communication were identified. Though I am considered an American trained intellectual at "home," my twelve-years of public schooling and four years of college education in Taiwan paved a foundation for my spherical, meandering, and conceptual approach to communication. Simultaneously, my intellectual training in CFE offers me a language of critique that troubles the view of education as accumulation of disciplinary knowledge. In a profound manner it challenges me to practice the philosophical understanding of knowledge as socially and politically constructed. Thus, what I consider an aesthetic and sophisticated way of thinking and communicating was pointed out, in evaluations, as a block that reduced and stalled comprehensibility and rendered my remarks unintelligible to my students, who I consider to be part of a "diversity" generation. By diversity generation, I mean a cohort that has grown up in the U.S. social and formal educational era that is landmarked by the motto of valuing "what diversity can offer." These students did not seem to appreciate an approach to teaching that differed from the norm.

We certainly could stop here and frame this educational tale as a successful/failed learning and teaching experience or about liking/disliking the course. Nonetheless, queer pedagogy and location theories won't allow us to take this easy way out, and here is how this intersectional framework insists on and contributes to making "diversity pedagogy" a more substantive and engaging endeavor. Deborah Britzman (1995) argues that knowledge and ignorance are not necessarily binaries, but "mutually implicate each other, structuring and enforcing particular forms of knowledge and forms of ignorance" (p. 3). In other words, ignorance should be analyzed "as an effect of knowledge, indeed as its limit, and not as an originary or innocent state" (p. 3). Therefore, ignorance is less about "not knowing," but more about "in/comprehensibility" or "un/intelligibility," i.e., what "normalcy can and cannot bear to know" (p. 3-4). While this student's evaluation was observant and

did take note of two different patterns of communication, her/his insistence on valuing the linear and the procedural attests to how differences are structured and evaluated through the dialectic of knowledge and ignorance. The "knowledge" that the evaluator already possesses serves "as an entitlement to [his/her] ignorance" of the "knowledge" that disrupts, rather than conforms to, the familiar, the norm.

Investigating the grounds of the thinkable is important to pedagogy. In the process of writing this essay, I became more mindful not only of how I thought, but also how my thinking informed my classroom pedagogy and how different and seemingly innocent pedagogical preferences were regulated by the structure of knowledge. I realized that I preferred to direct students' discussion more like a patch work and avoided an antagonistic model of communicating and conclusive, dichotomous debates in class discussions. I found myself struggling with my tolerance and appreciation of ambiguities and uncertainties, when students frequently asked for finite definitions, clear-cut answers, and technical and procedural instructions. These epistemological differences have consequences, and at the same time, they are the consequences of educational, cultural, and political processes. Britzman postulates, "Queer

29

Theory is an attempt to move away from psychological explanations like homophobia, which individualizes heterosexual fear of and loathing toward gay and lesbian subjects at the expense of examining how heterosexuality becomes normalized and natural" (p. 3). It offers a method of critique and an analytical tool to "mark the repetitions of normalcy as a structure and as a pedagogy" (p. 3).

In this essay, I use biographical encounters as evidential inquiry in the hope of going beyond the particularities of personal experiences. In a concrete and minute manner, I intend to expose norms to inquiry and consider them problematic. Drawing from Queer Theory which attends the reproductive and productive power of education, I strive, with this writing, to understand diversity work as an epistemic operation, not simply the "right thing to do," by using narratives to engage emergent identity as a possible access to multiple understandings of our shared social, educational realities. As a migrant intellectual worker in a prestigious, private, research university, I constantly find myself engulfed, yet awakened by the intertwined senses of empowerment, privilege, marginalization and injustice. These feelings and awareness, intimately felt, yet culturally, intellectually, and professionally mediated, serve as a critical lens to (re)read the complexity, subtlety,

Voices

Getting to know my LGBT peers and instructors, talking with them, taking classes with them, and having many discussions on LGBT issues has made me think and change.

>SU undergraduate student

and entrenchment of normativity as it is embedded within social, educational, and institutional encounters. They also function as a pedagogical and political site for struggle, engagement, and action.

I certainly hope my audiences are sophisticated enough not to dismiss or pigeonhole this account simply based on my deliberate act of foregrounding "migrant intellectual" as a material subject of personal and institutional histories and experiences. The normalizing regimes pertaining to race, class, gender, sexuality, ability, and geopolitical spatialization shape not only my subject location and movement, but actually inform how all of us are differentially positioned by, and position ourselves within, the conceptual, economic, and geopolitical webs of the global and local relations. This essay serves as one of many points of contact, alongside other disjunctures, between us. My narrative is not located in a "separate space" from your agencies. Here, as I think through how the way that I theorize diversity-linked pedagogical experience and subjectivity in relation to institutional practices, power relations, and the politics of knowledge frames the stories I told, I invite you to construct your own pedagogical experiences. Pedagogical narratives are central to diversity pedagogy which is intended to promote critical and political thinking and action. They have the potential to situate differing readings and versions of realities within the complexities and contradictions of educational and historical lives. They are the "tales of the field" (VanMaanen, 1988) that connect a historical and contextual understanding of our social locations to the theorization of the politics of knowledge, and to classroom practices that bare and re-configure the structure of meanings and intelligibility informing an uncritical pedagogy.

>>REFERENCES

Bell, S., Morrow, M., & Tastsoglou, E. (1999). Teaching in environments of resistance: Toward a critical, feminist, and antiracist pedagogy. In M. Maybery & E.C. Rose (Eds.), *Meeting the challenge: Innovative feminist pedagogies in action,* 23-48. NY: Routledge.

Britzman, D. (1995). Is there a queer pedagogy? Or, stop reading straight. *Educational Theory, 45* (2), 1-17.

Cervenak, S., Cespedes, K., Souza, C., & Straub, A. (2002). Imagining differently: The politics of listening in a feminist classroom. In Anzaldua & Keating (Eds.), *This bridge we call home,* 341-56. NY: Routledge.

Collin, P. H. (1990). *Black feminist thought: Knowledge, consciousness and the politics of empowerment.* NY: Routledge.

Delpit, L. D. (1988). The silenced dialogue: Power and pedagogy in educating other people's children. *Harvard Educational Review, 58*(3), 280-298.

Kaplan, C. (1996). *Questions of travel: Postmodern discourse of displacement.* Durham, NC: Duke University Press.

CONTINUED>>

Mohanty, C. T. (2003, March). *Cross-cultural, transnational feminist theories.* Paper presented to Women's Studies Program, Syracuse University.

Sarup, M. (1994). Home and identity. In Robertson, G., Marsh, M., Tisckner, L., Bird, J., Curtis, B., Putnam, T. (Eds.), *Travelers' tales: Narratives of home and displacement,* 93-104). New York: Routledge.

VanMaanen, J. (1988). *Tales of the field: On writing ethnography.* Chicago: University of Chicago Press.

The Invisible Presence of Sexuality in the Classroom

Ahoura Afshar

S hould discussions of sexuality be included in the classroom?[1] The easy answer might be no: it is not 'relevant' to the subject matter of most courses except perhaps to those that explicitly engage with human sexuality, such as Child and Family Studies, Sociology, or Women's Studies. Moreover, this reasoning might go, given estimates that within the general population less than ten percent identify as non-heterosexual, there's a good chance that in a class of sixty students everyone is straight.

It is this kind of perspective, however, that not only contributes to the invisibility of LGBT students, but it also constructs and reinforces heteronormativity in our classrooms and across campus.[2] LGBT students (and teachers) ARE present in our classrooms—whether we choose to see them or not—and it is their very *invisible presence* that demonstrates the power of heteronormativity to mask that which does not conform, and to naturalize that which does. This is a problem for both LGBT and heterosexual students and teachers alike. Heteronormative assumptions and practices regulate the beliefs, behaviors, and desires of ALL of us, restricting the range of possibilities of identification and expression for ALL of us, to such an extent that even momentary and joyful expressions (e.g. the heterosexual man singing "I feel like a woman" in the Chevy commercial discussed by Susan Adams) become sources of discomfort and fear.

Practices of regulation and restriction are integral to creating and maintaining hierarchies of power, which in turn limit the kinds of learning and teaching that can happen in our classrooms. As responsible teachers, we know that our pedagogical theories and practices need to expand the kinds of learning opportunities we provide students, not restrict them. In fact, the administration of this university recognizes the importance of this by emphasizing the link between a rich intellectual climate and a diversity of perspectives and people: "[. . .] diversity in our student body, faculty, and staff has far-ranging and significant educational benefits for *all* non-minorities and minorities alike" (Syracuse University Academic Plan, 2001). Particular strategies to create more inclusive curricula have been developed and implemented in programs and departments university-wide because "[s]tudents in diverse learning environments learn more, and have higher

Voices

Airing and understanding multiple perspectives is a procedure for building knowledge together, rather than a morally charged contest for truth and correctness.

>Marjorie DeVault
(DeVault, 1999)

levels of satisfaction and greater degrees of civic engagements. They are better able to appreciate the ideas of others and they are better prepared to enter the world they will lead" (SU Academic Plan, 2001). This diversity of students, faculty, and ideas includes: "race, ethnicity, gender, age, religious beliefs, *sexual orientation*, and physical and mental ability" (Syracuse University Human Resources, emphasis added).

In principle, then, SU values diversity. Taking a closer look at what diversity means and how it is "practiced," however, exposes some gaps between these principles and actual, everyday classroom procedures, particularly when that "diversity" topic is sexual orientation. It's important to note that sexual orientation is a term that does not reference a particular set of people; it's not only about LGBT people, but also non-LGBT, or heterosexual, people. Why is this broader definition of sexual orientation important? Because the sexual orientation of heterosexuality is simultaneously institutionalized and naturalized to the extent that it becomes the invisible norm against which all other sexual orientations, identifications, or expressions are named "abnormal." The issue of "invisibility," then, isn't just about LGBT students and teachers; it's about the ways in which our assumptions about (hetero)sexuality are invisible to us. And we carry these assumptions into our classrooms. As a result, heteronormativity is reproduced, most often unconsciously, through our own everyday classroom practices. Rather than expanding the kinds of learning opportunities we create space for, we inadvertently reinforce a regulated and restrictive framework for understanding the complexity of human sexuality.

II. Ten years ago, research with Syracuse University LGBT students showed that one third of the respondents would have gone to another school had they had sufficient information on the circumstances surrounding LGBT issues on campus (Sherrill & Hardesty, 1994).

Although the situation has changed since then, this statistic may still be accurate to some degree. Bias against those who are perceived to bend the rules of heteronormative behavior pervades SU's campus climate. There are still cases of verbal abuse and physical attacks against LGBT students on this campus: instances of name-calling, of derogatory comments written on doors, dry-erase boards, or computer desktops in residence halls and on campus, and even of physical assault on the basis of perceived sexual orientation (Syracuse University Public Safety, 2004; see also Byrnes, 2003; Wightman, 2003). "Fifty-one percent of bias-related incidents reported last fall [2003] had to do with sexual orientation, while 27 percent concerned gender" (Moritz, 2004). These statistics show that many LGBT students face problems that their straight peers do not. Non-straight students often experience a complex process that involves questioning their sexual orientation, achieving a comfortable sexual identity, coming out, and self-acceptance. They often experience loneliness, isolation, and exclusion in this process. And, they are often targets of homophobia simply because the heterosexual majority claims an exclusive version of sexuality and morality due to the regulative powers of heteronorms. Despite these facts, there is silence in our classrooms when it comes to sexuality. It appears as if no one wants to recognize this silence as a problem, let alone discuss ways of addressing it. Why?

>>linked>>>>>>>>>>>>>>>>>>>>>>>>>>>

LGBT/Queer Studies Websites >>
www.public.iastate.edu/~savega/les_biga.htm

Extensive directory that includes selected LGBT web resources useful for academic research and information purposes.

One reason there are so many misconceptions about sexuality is that it is not talked about in U.S. educational systems. It is not generally included in primary schools because, it is argued, it is too early for children to learn about sexuality (Fine, 1988). It is often not included in high school curricula because, the argument goes, adolescents are at a crucial age and should not be exposed to the "promotion of sexuality," especially non-heterosexuality. It is not included in college since it is not 'relevant' to the subject matter in most courses. But, sexuality is relevant: it is not just about sex; it is a critical aspect of life, a primary means through which we identify ourselves, though this identification is usually unconscious for people who identify as "heterosexual" because heterosexuality is the assumed norm, and thus invisible as a "marker" of identity. For LGBT-identified people, however, sexuality is a conscious "marker" of identity; describing oneself in terms such as "gay," "lesbian," "bisexual," "transgender," or "queer" is fundamental to the process of "coming out." Thus, sexuality is not simply a "private" aspect of individuals, but is intimately connected with power relations in our culture, and influences much of our social experiences. There is much misinformation and bias regarding matters of sexuality. There are students with "non-traditional" sexual identities whose needs are not usually met. Only a tiny fraction of the entire student body may take courses that directly address sexuality and the privileges it awards, denies, and limits access to, and hence the majority of students will never discuss the politics of sexuality in any classroom. But it is a mistake to think that this is a problem only for LGBT students.

A social stigma has been attached to sexualities other than heterosexuality, bred out of the myths and misinformation this volume is trying to "interrupt." Hence, some people find moral justification in being violent towards non-straights. Emphasizing the shamefulness of same-sex desire, this logic simply ignores the fact that most people have some sort of "non-heterosexual" fantasy or experience at some point in their lifetime (Laumann et. al., 1994). One may have such experiences without having a LGBT orientation. Being unaware of such facts may cause heterosexuals to experience these fantasies with immeasurable anxiety, dreading that they might be gay.

Gay-bashing may also be seen as a way of proving one's masculinity. The pressure to "prove one's heterosexual manhood" can lead to the need to disparage gays in all ways. This kind of sexual stereotyping not only encourages violence against those who are perceived to be LGBT, but also causes psychological dissonance for straight youth, who are endeavoring to comply with rigid gender roles. It is because of these rigid gender roles that sexuality is an issue that all students face, regardless of their sexual orientation.

III. Including discussions about sexuality in the classroom, however, does not necessarily mean that it has to be part of the syllabus of each course. What's important to acknowledge and make visible is that heteronormativity is present, even if invisible, in all our classroom interactions: in student-student and student-teacher pre- and post-class banter, and in students' and teachers' physical and verbal behaviors. For example, engineering student Alex Chapeaux describes how a professor's "innocent"

question about his girlfriend compelled Alex to tell this professor that he didn't have one. When the professor prodded him for an explanation, Alex replied: "I [am] looking for a boyfriend" (Rupp, et.al., 2004). Chapeaux observes that "now she is more careful about what she says in front of me" (Rupp, et.al., 2004). In addition to our interactions with students, we need to pay attention to how heteronormativity shapes the scenarios and examples we use to explain material. For instance, in a course on statistics an example that uses "married couples" ignores the fact that non-heterosexual marriage is not legalized or recognized in many places, and that this kind of example simply reinforces heterosexual privilege. An alternate example might be just as effective: "What would be the effect of civil unions for LGBT people on birth rates?" This simple

The issue of "invisibility," then, isn't just about LGBT students and teachers; it's about the ways in which <our assumptions> about (hetero)sexuality are invisible to us.

but profoundly important change in language interrupts heteronormativity while also affirming that sexuality is a complicated issue. In a language course, an instructor should be sensitive to usage of pronouns: maybe it is not an accident that a bloke refers to 'he' as his partner. Should a student have to come out to the class or to the teacher if she simply wants to describe her girlfriend in an assignment? In most courses, and on most topics, instructors can construct effective examples and problems using non-conventional subjects. For instance, you could ask, "if Dave and Bob want to buy a $200,000 house but only make $25,000 annually, how should they budget?" Or, "how are the histories of the gay rights movement and the African-American movement linked?"[3] Or, "what is the most efficient building design for non-gender-specific dorms?" These small, but significant, changes acknowledge the presence of LGBT-identified students, and create a more inclusive and effective learning environment. SU student Matt Ward comments: "It is important to see yourself reflected in what is around you" (Rupp, et.al., 2004). Beyond being consciously aware of and working to interrupt heteronormative assumptions in class assignments, TAs and professors should be sensitive to the effects of a hostile environment on LGBT students' academic work. For example, if a student fails to finish an assignment because she or he has been experiencing stress and anxiety due to homophobia and heterosexism in the dorms, the instructor should take into consideration the legitimacy of this excuse.

If issues of sexuality are brought up in a discussion, then view this as an opportunity to talk about it in the classroom. There is a great need to discuss sexuality in a "safe" but critical environment where we can work with students to interrogate the "facts" they've learned about sexual diversity through the images and languages that dominate the media and other social institutions, and show them alternative views. It is often in college when students form a stable sexual identity and LGBT students have their first

expressions

SEXUAL IDENTITY

>>>one's personal sense of sexual orientation (and the names people use to refer to it)

"coming out" experience (D'Augelli, as cited in Eddy and Forney, 2000). Some students may experience their friends' or peers' coming out and may have questions about it. Some may also be under pressure to comply with rigid gender roles that are expected from them. In addition, because heteronormativity affects all people—LGBT or straight—failing to consider these issues further silences the topic of sexuality. Rather than limiting our perspective to issues of bias or violence against perceived or LGBT-identified individuals, we must understand that, as SU Professor Barbara Applebaum points out, "a lot of [...] students feel that homophobia just means hate, fear, taboo, and they don't understand how they are complicit in keeping the norm of heteronormativity in place. Because they are not homophobic. They don't hate. They don't fear. So unless you also teach them about the norm of heterosexualism then they don't get what the problem is. They don't see the bigger picture."[4] This norm limits the range of sexual expressions for straight students as well as LGBT-identified students.

We need to recognize that our role as educators affects students and issues they are dealing with, and address such issues that are generally left out of our class discussions. We can make use of different opportunities—discussions of local events, lectures that present a range of relationships, assignments structured to connect students' everyday lives with abstract concepts—that arise to create spaces in the curriculum and classroom for perspectives that bend rigid heteronormative views and interrogate the power relations inherent in these views. This can help students understand that difference in sexual identities or orientations is a fact in an environment of great diversity. From this perspective, everyone can learn from differences found in ourselves and others. This is the responsibility of all employees at Syracuse University: to create and sustain an academic and social environment in which diversity in all its dimensions is valued.

>>The author would like to thank Mary Queen for help with substantial revisions.

>>REFERENCES

Byrnes, E. (2003). Syracuse University's anti-bias protocol precedes and ensures compliance with legislation recently signed into law [Electronic version]. Retrieved April 5, 2004 from http://sunews.syr.edu/fullstory.asp?id=923039

DeVault, M. (1999). *Liberating method: Feminism and social research.* Philadelphia: Temple University Press.

Eddy, W., & Forney, D. (2000). Assessing campus environments for the lesbian, gay and bisexual population. In Wall & Evans (Eds.), *Toward acceptance: Sexual orientation issues on campus.* Lanham, MD: University Press of America.

Faludi, S. (1999). *Stiffed: The betrayal of the American man.* New York: William Morrow and Co.

Fine, M. (1988). Sexuality, schooling and adolescent females: The missing discourse of desire. *Harvard Educational Review 58*(1) 29-53.

Laumann, E., Gagne, J., Michael, R., & Michaels, S. (1994). *The social organization of sexuality.* Chicago: University of Chicago Press.

Moritz, C. (2004). *SU reports, responds to bias incidents* [Electronic Version]. Retrieved April 5, 2004 from http://sunews.syr.edu/fullstory.asp?id=3230408

Rupp, A., Becker, M., Monge, E. French, & Ricardi, A. (2004). 'Climate' varies across campus. *Student Voice, ix* (21), 12, 34.

Sherrill, J.- M., & Hardesty, C. (1994). *The gay, lesbian, and bisexual students' guide to colleges, universities and graduate schools.* New York: New York University Press.

Syracuse University Academic Plan. (2001). A strategic partnership for innovative research and education (A-SPIRE): An academic plan for Syracuse University [Electronic version]. Retrieved April 29, 2004 from http://provost.syr.edu/academicplan/april2001.asp

CONTINUED>>

Syracuse University Human Resources. (n.d.). Diversity at S.U. [Electronic version]. Retrieved April 30, 2004 from http://humanresources.syr.edu/support/diversty.html

Syracuse University Public Safety (2004). *Daily Crime Logs* [Electronic version]. Retrieved from http://publicsafety.syr.edu/MediaLog1.html

Wightman, R. (2003). Letter: SU campus coursing with gender bias [Electronic version]. *Daily Orange*, October 30, 2003.

>>ENDNOTES

1 > This essay uses various terms—sexuality, sexual orientation, sexual identity—that are distinct from each other, but linked by structures of heteronormativity. The two former terms can refer to sexual practices and/or sexual identity, while the latter term generally refers to how an individual self-identifies. This essay used "sexuality" as an umbrella term for a range of sexual practices and/or sexual identities, including heterosexuality. The term "gender," on the other hand, refers to sets of behaviors/identifications that are attributed (by social norms) to females and males. Thus, gender cannot be conflated with sexuality, although it is intricately linked with it. For more specific definitions of each, please refer to the "Glossary" in this volume.

2 > Please see the essay in this volume by Susan Adams for more on heteronormativity.

3 > I owe these examples to Dean Allbritton.

4 > From interview with Barbara Applebaum in Part II of this volume.

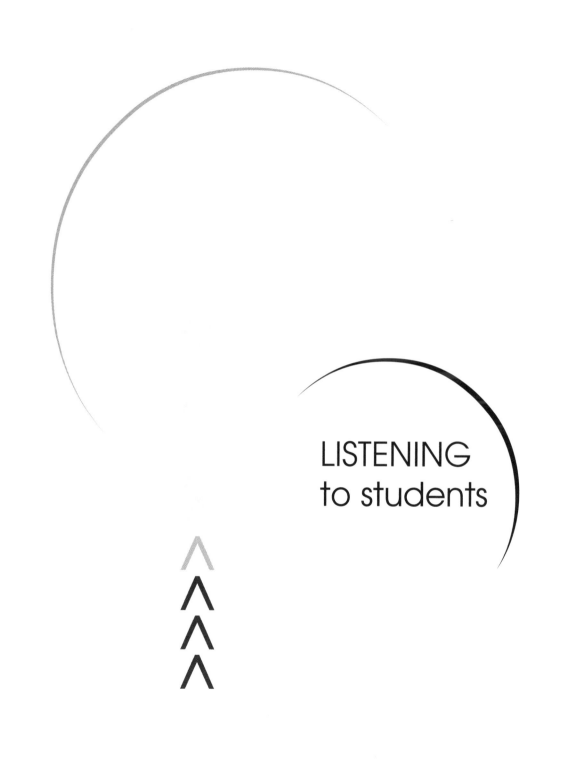

LISTENING
to students

(Un)Straightening the Syracuse University Landscape

Aman Luthra

"Stay in your closets" was just one of several hateful messages chalked on the SU sidewalks during Coming Out Week in October 2000 (Blum, 2000; Davia, 2000). These anti-gay chalkings on the quad sparked considerable controversy within the SU campus community, but this is not the only instance in which the quad has acted as a space where conflicts between LGBT-supportive and non-supportive students find violent expression. It is with a particular series of incidents involving the use of visible spaces on the SU campus that I seek to alert the reader to the intersections between sexuality and space, particularly the relationship between heteronormativity and the visible landscape of SU.[1] How is sexuality embedded within the landscape? How does the visible landscape, particularly the SU campus, embody, privilege, and reproduce heteronormative social relations? I suggest that struggles over sexuality—made visible on the concrete spaces of the landscape (such as the sidewalks on the SU campus quad)—can, on the one hand, be

45

representative of broader conflicts about sexuality within society and, on the other, serve as historic moments in defining social relations and longer-term institutional responses to these struggles.

Why should you be interested in reading this essay? Why does the landscape matter to anybody? For graduate students, faculty, and administrators who might not otherwise engage with these issues intellectually, I suggest the following reasons for reading this essay. First, drawing upon a lively literature on the landscape (both in its representations and its material form) within cultural geography, I suggest that it is important to not view the visible landscape at face value. The landscape necessarily needs to be understood as a product of the social relations that it embodies and reproduces (Mitchell, 2000). In other words, normative understandings of the landscape can lead to the reproduction of heteronormative discourses that continually make the landscape an inhospitable space for those who do not conform to its assumptions, i.e. the queer community. If we view the landscape at face value, not only do we uncritically accept its assumptions but we also play a part in reproducing and perpetuating its privilege. Therefore we, as teachers of a wide range of students, need to be cognizant of and perceptive about how

...because the policy is AMBIGUOUS, heteronormativity <gets> INSTITUTIONALIZED.

these embedded discourses relate to their lives, and our own. Second, once we recognize the importance of the visible landscape in embodying and reproducing heterosexual privilege, we can be active in creating spaces for the articulation of alternative discourses. These 'safe spaces' that allow for the existence of alternative sexualities are critical to the successful maintenance of a diverse campus community.

Several scholars have written extensively about the relationships between sexuality and space. My purpose in this particular essay is not simply to summarize and reiterate the brilliant insights that these works have provided, but to use them to provide an alternative reading of the SU landscape. Designed space has often acted as "a regulator of public and private realms" and the "collusion of architecture in [a] ruse of heterosexual mythology is now well recognized" (Ingram, Bouthillette, & Retter, 1997, p. 374-5). The design of the American suburb, for instance, has been related to the entrenchment of patriarchal and heterosexual norms within society (Coontz, 1992; Ingram et. al., 1997). Indeed the critical role that the built landscape can play in shaping identities is a point that outgoing Chancellor Kenneth Shaw also recognizes in a letter that prefaces the walking tour guide of campus:

> This is a campus shaped by students' needs and desires. The 170 major buildings, the quadrangles, the walkways, the hills, and the playing field are far more than solid realities. They have had a part in forming each of our students' experiences. They are rich in memories. This is also a place where a vision has taken hold. Our physical environment is designed to help make that so (Syracuse University, n.d.).

Much as the "University's history is embedded in the campus itself" (Syracuse University, n.d., 3), so are unspoken assumptions about sexuality. One does not have to look too far beyond the seemingly apolitical process of the allocation of students to rooms in residence halls or even the design of locker rooms in the gymnasium, both of which assume heterosexuality, to infer a narrative of sexual norms that are built into our physical environment. To this end, in the following sections, I will alert the reader to the conflicts that can result when assumed sexual norms are transgressed in the physical spaces of the landscape, and the ways in which these struggles can lead to potentially emancipatory outcomes.

Chalkings and hosings on the quad: Sexuality and public space

This section examines two different sets of incidents both involving the representation of alternative sexualities on the concrete sidewalks that crisscross the SU campus quad. The first involves an institutional response in the form of cleaning, or hosing away, pro-gay messages chalked on the quad by LGBT members of the SU community during the Coming Out Week celebrations in October 1997.[2] The second is a more direct conflict expressed in the form of anti-gay messages that were written on the quad in response to the chalked pro-gay messages during Coming Out Week in October 2000.

"SU erases chalkings: Physical Plant hoses Coming Out Week messages on Quad" reads the headline of an article in the October 8, 1997 issue of the *Daily*

Orange (Akin & Barton, 1997, p. 1). During Coming Out Week in October 1997, gay-pride messages such as "I'm a dyke" and "There is a fag in Newhouse" were erased by SU Physical Plant after they allegedly received complaints from students and faculty regarding the "offensive" nature of these messages. Several members of the SU community suggested that cleaning of gay-pride chalkings was unnecessary censorship that would only perpetuate homophobia on campus. Despite this, Physical Plant erased Coming Out Week chalkings again the following day. Shawn Adam, Assistant Director for Administration at the Physical Plant, and Robert Hill, Vice-President for Public Relations, both agreed that the 'hosings' were justified on the pretext that they had received complaints from students and faculty (Barton, 1997). The whole incident concluded under an ambiguous justification of "policy problems" and resulted in a letter to the University community from Barry Wells, the Vice President for Student Affairs and Dean of Student Relations of the University, apologizing for the confusion and reaffirming the University's commitment to diversity. The University's use of a regulatory apparatus, the Physical Plant, in this 'hosing' incident needs to be understood as an attempt by the University to create and sustain a particular kind of order in its visible landscape—an order that is inordinately heteronormative and anti-gay.

Three years later, in October 2000, anti-gay chalkings on the quad read: "We're mad and will be silent no more;" "Be gay and pay;" "Stand up and stop the gay community from shoving their beliefs on us;" "Keep the gay shit to yourself;" "I don't need to know who you fuck" (Blum, 2000). Aside from simply being messages expressing hatred and violence, these words chalked on the quad also need to be understood as aggressive acts of resistance to the use of public space by a social minority group who attempted to claim rights to publicly express their identities. These writings were a response to the prideful Coming Out Week chalkings, inviting the SU campus community to come out, celebrate with, and be a part of SU's queer community.

Xpressions

HOMOPHOBIA

>>>belief that LGBT people don't deserve the same rights as people who aren't LGBT; fear and hatred of "homosexuals"

48

Chalkings on the quad by the queer community visibly distorted a "straight" landscape. These distortions are precisely what elicited an aggressive response that attempted to reaffirm the dominant heterosexual paradigm of the visible landscape by suppressing the expression of alternative sexualities.

In a spontaneous interview with Leon Blum, Chancellor Shaw commented on this incident: "[…] the important thing is to not view this as an organized movement" (Blum, 2000). What makes a movement organized? By no means are these acts of hatred *random*; not only are they systematic but also they are routinely structured by a dominant discourse. Inasmuch as heteronormative discourses are embedded in institutions, policies, and our mundane daily practices, then they are indeed *organized*. Both of these incidents reveal the assumed straightness of the SU campus. In the first incident, because the policy is ambiguous, heteronormativity gets institutionalized. In the second incident, underlying straightness finds expression in the aggressive reactions of the perpetrators. Both of these incidents also tell us a story about the use and governance of public space at SU. If we regard the quad as public space (at least within the context of

the University), we imagine that the entire SU community has access to it. As is evident through the chalking incidents, however, access is far from free. Instead, it is structured through cultural norms and legal practices that institutionalize and privilege particular social relations within the community.

Since these two incidents, the SU campus has seen rather significant changes with regards to its relations vis-à-vis the LGBT community. Following a request from the Senate Student Life Committee to the Senate Agenda Committee for the appointment of an Ad Hoc Committee on LGBT Concerns, filed in March 1998, such a committee was established. The committee's purpose includes assessing the concerns of SU's LGBT community, and making recommendations for the University's responses to these concerns. The committee has since been granted permanent status. In addition, a LGBT resource center has also been established. In the year 2000-2001, the University Senate Committee on Budget and Fiscal

Affairs allocated a budget of $90,000 to the LGBT Resource Center. Despite these praiseworthy developments, the SU landscape continues to embody and privilege heteronormative social relations.

"Too aggressive and political": Sexuality and the cultural landscape of SU

The quad is not the only space to which access is governed by generally accepted heteronormative cultural norms within the SU community. Heterosexual privilege pervades all aspects of everyday life on the SU campus. It is precisely for this reason that the undergraduate LGBT student group on campus was criticized for being "too aggressive and political" by some members of both the straight and LGBT community (Akin, 1998). Pride Union, the undergraduate LGBT group, has to constantly balance between acting as a safe space for undergraduates and being an aggressive LGBT activist group. If sexuality and everyday life did not intersect constantly in complicated ways, Pride Union wouldn't have to manage such a formidable task. Those who criticized Pride Union for being "too aggressive and political" are disturbed by the group's sexual transgressions on the SU cultural landscape.

Bulletin boards and restrooms are just some of the other elements of the visible landscape that are frequent sites of LGBT-supportive and non-supportive conflicts at SU. Bulletin boards, especially in residence halls, are sites where such a conflict can be witnessed on almost a daily basis. In fact, a majority of the bias-related incidents reported to the Dean of Student's office involve derogatory remarks regarding the perceived sexual orientation of the victims, written on the visible spaces of bulletin boards and whiteboards on individual students' rooms. Once again, heternormativity is not restricted to the realm of popular culture, manifested in such everyday conflicts, but is embodied in the institutional regulatory practices as well. The following incident involving the vandalism of gay pride posters provides evidence in this regard. Akin (1998) notes, "gay pride posters were ripped down by members of the Office of Residence Life because they depicted scenes of half-naked underwear models and girls kissing girls" (p. 3). Another student notes, "the simple act of putting up 'safe space' stickers [. . .] has brought her grief" (Flynn, 2002, p. 25).[3] The student continues, "[m]onths ago a group of men saw the sticker on her bedroom window late at night and began banging on her window, yelling and screaming derogatory slurs at her" (Flynn, 2002, p. 25). As recent as fall 2003, Coming Out Week posters were torn down from buildings all over campus upon complaints from some members of the SU community regarding the provocative nature of these posters (Kaechele, 2003). Much like the quad, bulletin boards are also sites within the visible landscape where heteronormative relations at SU become institutionalized through cultural norms (for instance, through hate messages) as well as policy-based practices (for instance, the removal of Coming Out Week posters by the University).

Creating progressive political spaces

In a letter addressed to the SU community, dated February 14, 2003, SU's Team Against Bias noted that, in Fall 2003, almost 73% of bias-related incidents reported to the Office of the Dean of Students were based on actual, or perceived, sexual orientation or gender identity. In a report by the University's Ad Hoc Committee on Gay, Lesbian, Bisexual and Transgender Concerns, dated May 2001, the authors note that a survey of the campus community (students, faculty, staff, and administrators) showed that LGBT respondents were less likely to view the representations of LGBT community as neutral than non-LGBT respondents. While LGBT persons at SU perceived queer representations in campus media (*Daily Orange* and *Syracuse Record*) as negative, other SU community members perceived them as neutral. Finally, the report also suggested that LGBT students considered the University to be far less

VOICES

I think a real issue on campus is that people who don't identify as LGBT feel that LGBT issues have absolutely no relationship to them.

>SU undergraduate student

committed to making the campus safe for LGBT persons than non-LGBT respondents. What I have been arguing in this paper is that the visible landscape has much to do with these divergent perceptions and understandings of the LGBT community here at SU. By briefly exploring sexual politics on visible spaces of the campus, I hope to have elucidated some of the mechanisms by which the campus landscape becomes a product of heteronormative social relations within the SU community, and shown that such a landscape becomes an inhospitable space for those who do not conform to its assumptions.

Contemporary institutional practices, inasmuch as they embody popular cultural norms, will continue to reproduce a landscape that is more welcoming to straight rather than LGBT students unless a concerted effort is made to make visible those aspects of the landscape that question its heterosexual assumptions. Although the struggles over space, as witnessed in the quad incidents, reveal a dark period in SU history, these incidents were also a defining moment for a recognition and institutionalization of more progressive sexual politics by our administration. Recent increased visibility of the queer community in the campus media, and the establishment of the LGBT Resource Center and the University Senate Committee on LGBT Concerns are some crucial steps in the creation of spaces that

allow for the articulation of alternative sexualities. Indeed, these steps are also associated with an increased visibility of the LGBT community in campus media and on campus at large. These are certainly progressive transformations in SU's institutional and cultural landscape. But much remains to be done and a critical engagement with the landscape can be a primary step in this direction. As educators, it is our responsibility to shed light upon the assumptions subsumed within the visible landscape. Through classroom discussions as well personal conversations with students, we must not only point out these assumptions but also be active in making sure that they are violated so that *concrete* safe spaces can be created on the campus.

>>The author would like to thank Laam Hae, a Ph.D. candidate in the Department of Geography at Syracuse University, for suggesting this title: "(Un)Straightening the SU landscape."

>>References

Akin, P. (1998, December 11). Gay community ponders climate, resources. *Daily Orange*, 3.

Akin, P. & Barton, N. (1997, October 8). SU erases chalkings. *Daily Orange*, 1, 4.

CONTINUED>>

Barton, N. (1997, October 9). Quad gets hosed again. *Daily Orange*, 1, 5.

Blum, L. (2000). *Chalk.* (VHS Recording). Available at the Syracuse University LGBT Resource Center, 750 Ostrom Avenue, Syracuse, NY 13244-4350.

Coontz, S. (1992). *The way we never were: American families and the nostalgia trap.* New York: Basic Books.

Davia, J. (2000, October 13). Anti-gay group chalks quad. *Daily Orange,* 1, 8.

Flynn, A. (2002, February 25). Gay students excluded in heterosexual classroom. *Daily Orange*, 20, 25.

Horseman, J. (1997, February 7). Pride Union launches 'safe' program. *Daily Orange*, 1, 6.

Ingram, G., Bouthillette, A., & Retter, Y. (1997). *Queers in space: Communities, public places, sites of resistance.* Seattle: Bay Press.

Kaechele, J. (2003, September 26). Gay posters promote awareness. *Daily Orange*.

Mitchell, D. (2000). *Cultural geography: A critical introduction.* Malden: Blackwell Publishers.

Syracuse University. (n.d.). *A walking tour: Syracuse University.* [Brochure] Syracuse, NY: Syracuse University.

Syracuse University Senate Ad Hoc Committee on Gay, Lesbian, Bisexual and Transgendered Concerns. (March 21, 2003). Report and Recommendations. (Available from Syracuse University LGBT Resource Center, 750 Ostrom Avenue, Syracuse, NY 13244).

>>ENDNOTES

1 > For a definition and discussion of the concept of heteronormativity, see the essay by Susan Adams in this volume.

2 > Coming Out Week is a week of events aimed at creating awareness of LGBT issues and is hosted on the SU campus in the early part of the Fall semester every year.

CONTINUED>>

3 > Safe Space stickers are a part of the Safe Space Campaign started in 1997, sponsored by the Rainbow Alliance, Pride Union and Open Doors. A Safe Space symbol is not an indicator of sexuality but provides the assurance that a non-hostile environment will be provided to anyone regardless of his or her sexuality (Horseman 1997).

Echoes of Silence:
Experiences of LGBT College Students at Syracuse University

Rachel Moran and Brian Stout

Although the following conversation is fictitious, the details are not. We constructed this essay as a dialogue to portray a realistic conversation that might occur between two LGBT students at Syracuse University. Although we do not speak on behalf of all LGBT students on campus, we sincerely attempt to tell some of their actual stories, experiences, and thoughts in an effort to "break the silence" that continues to oppress LGBT students at Syracuse University.

It's a cold Tuesday night in September. Two S.U. students bump into each other on Marshall Street and decide to get lattes at Starbucks.

BRIAN: So, how's it going?

RACHEL: Not so great actually. Did you read the D.O. today?

BRIAN: Yeah, why?

RACHEL: It said that there was an anti-gay hate crime last weekend.

BRIAN: Oh… yeah I know about it.

RACHEL: It really surprised me. I know this isn't the most accepting college campus out there, but I never expected anything like this to happen here.

BRIAN: Yeah, me neither. I mean, being a freshman, I've only been a student here for about 2 weeks, but I had always assumed that people on a college campus would be pretty accepting.

RACHEL: I guess I've had mixed experiences… I'm not really sure just how accepting it is here. I know you said before that when you were looking at colleges, you liked Syracuse because it seemed like a very diverse and accepting school. What made you think that?

BRIAN: Well, I had no idea exactly what to expect of SU before I came here. I had actually read in one book that profiled colleges around the country that there was a big divide between gay and straight students on this campus. The book said that there was a certain "tension" regarding LGBT issues here. That kind of scared me. On the other hand, I had done some research on my own. I was looking around the Internet to see what kind of LGBT resources Syracuse had to offer when I discovered the website for the LGBT Resource Center. I read about everything the Center had to offer, and was pretty impressed. I found the email address of the director, Adrea Jaehnig, and sent her an email regarding some of my reservations about coming here. She really made me feel a lot better. It's really great that we have an LGBT Resource Center on this campus. I know a lot of people who go to schools without any formal LGBT support organizations.

RACHEL: Yeah, the Center is amazing and Adrea does so much. But just the presence of the Center alone doesn't mean that the University is at ease with queer issues… after all, think about this hate crime.

BRIAN: You know, I really just don't want to talk about the hate crime right now... maybe later, okay? So anyway, how are your classes going so far?

RACHEL: Well, it's funny that we were just talking about whether or not SU is an accepting place. Even though I love my classes this semester, I keep finding myself in uncomfortable situations.

BRIAN: Really? Me, too. I was just in a class that covers progressive issues and we were talking about how gay people are oppressed. It was nice that nobody really said anything derogatory towards LGBT people, but all of the other guys felt compelled to keep saying things like "I'm straight," and "but I'm not gay" while talking about these issues. I was almost tempted to make up a girlfriend or something just so everyone wouldn't know I was gay. It was almost like I had to match up to their masculinity. I really felt like I wasn't good enough to give my opinions because I wasn't straight.

RACHEL: Yeah I hate how, sometimes, straight people who mean well and support the LGBT community are so scared of being identified as gay. But wait, I thought you were already out?

BRIAN: Well, I am, and I definitely wouldn't mind coming out in class, but I really didn't want it to be under those circumstances. When everybody is defending their own heterosexuality, it hardly feels like a comfortable place to come out. How have you gone about coming out in class?

RACHEL: Well, I guess it really depends on the class. I took French classes last year, and even though my TA seemed very liberal, as part of getting us to speak in French, she'd ask questions like "How would you describe your ideal boyfriend?" and "How would you describe your future plans for marriage and children?" I know it was unintentional, but it felt like my whole existence was erased. I've never cared about marriage or kids, but all of the sudden they were something I wasn't worthy of, something I was literally stripped of the vocabulary for. It was just a little vocabulary exercise, but I really didn't know what to do. In the end, I just went along with it trying to be as gender-neutral as possible to avoid marking myself as queer, but the whole exercise left me with a bad taste.

BRIAN: Really? I didn't think you would mind coming out in class.

RACHEL: Well, even though I have come out in some classes, we both know how hard it really can be.

BRIAN: Yeah, especially in classrooms that perpetuate such a heterosexual norm.

RACHEL: Exactly. Nobody wants to be known as "the gay kid." Then, the next time a LGBT issue comes up in class, everybody looks to you for an answer, as if you represent an entire group of people. In my poetry class last semester, I brought some poems that were gender-neutral, and almost immediately I was asked about my boyfriend. I was uncomfortable then, too, but it was a much smaller and friendlier setting, and I did correct their assumptions.

BRIAN: Wow... what did you say?

RACHEL: I actually told everyone that the poems were about a girl and then there was silence. But it was so stupid because everybody knows I'm queer. But I was really impressed with my professor because even before that, he really made a point of treating everybody's work as if it could be written by anybody and about anybody. Actually, this approach sometimes makes kids who aren't used to thinking about sexuality uncomfortable.

Brian: But when you think about it, that's something that we have to deal with every day.

RACHEL: Have you come out in any classes yet?

BRIAN: Well, I haven't actually said the words, "I'm gay," but I feel like it's pretty obvious by the stances I take on LGBT issues and how passionately I speak on behalf of gay rights in classes. For example, in my sociology class the other day, when people were talking about gay families with children, we talked about the misconception that gay parents will produce gay children. I think I really cleared up people's misconceptions when I pointed out that the "most common" way to produce a gay child is through heterosexual sex.

RACHEL: (laughs) Isn't it funny how when you don't qualify a passionate statement for gay rights with "I'm straight," people label you as gay? That's why I have so much respect for my straight friends who stand up for what they believe in and don't feel the need to point out or defend their own heterosexuality.

BRIAN: Yeah, I'm really surprised that teachers don't seem to notice when kids preface their statements with things like "Well, I'm straight, *but...* ." I think that would be a really great way to point out the prevalence of heteronormativity.

RACHEL: Yeah, and not to be a bitch, but you have to hear this one: I was doing a series of interviews for a class freshman year, and because my TA seemed pretty cool, I interviewed her as part of the project, only to find out that her "greatest challenge" is "dealing with" gay people. She knew it sounded awful, but she told me that gay people make her uncomfortable, and that unlike when she works with other minorities, she feels like she has to apologize to gay people for being straight. Not only did she assume that I was heterosexual, but she really shocked me with her ignorance.

BRIAN: She actually said that? Do straight people really think we want them to apologize for their sexuality? That's crazy!

RACHEL: Well, I certainly don't think she represents most straight people with her view. But the worst part was that she asked me to strike that comment from my notes and leave it out of the interview. Not wanting to cause her major trouble or wanting to risk my own grade, I complied with her request. Still, it has left an impression on me that I don't think I can ever forget.

BRIAN: Well did you at least eventually tell her that you were gay?

RACHEL: I kind of played the same game you played in sociology and more or less came out to my class the next week. I'm still not sure if she ever made the connection.

BRIAN: Did she ever apologize?

RACHEL: For being straight?

59

BRIAN: (laughs) No, for being ignorant.

RACHEL: No. She never mentioned it again. But I bet that if she did apologize, it would probably be for her heterosexuality, not her ignorance.

BRIAN: (laughs again)

RACHEL: But really, the fact that she never brought it up again says a lot about how invisible gay issues really are.

BRIAN: And I think that silence is one of the major hurdles that the LGBT community has to deal with. Unfortunately, people seem to underestimate the size of our community just because there are so many LGBT people who aren't visible or who aren't in a position where they can safely and comfortably speak out. In fact, just the other day, my friend came into my room all upset. When he was walking out of the dining hall, this guy in line started calling him a faggot and saying hurtful things to him about his sexual orientation. I felt like running back downstairs to find the guy. It was so heart breaking to me that out of probably 10 or 15 people in line, nobody was motivated to speak up. It's so difficult to be the only one defending yourself in that kind of situation. I was so surprised that my friend, who is totally open about his sexuality, didn't stand up for himself. Since nobody spoke up, how can we be sure that this boy won't say something like that again?

RACHEL: I know we're all guilty sometimes of letting comments slide by assuming that they are not supposed to be offensive. But it's hard to be the one to have to respond to every seemingly benign comment.

BRIAN: Yeah, it seems like a lot the time gay people are made to feel like they are being overly sensitive, but then again, it seems like most of the time, nobody else really steps up to the plate to speak out on their behalf when these things actually do happen. I know I've been at parties with my own friends where I overhear anti-gay slurs, but everyone just lets them slide by, including myself. I want to speak up, but it's so difficult to be the only one saying anything.

Rachel: Things like this happen every day, but come on, when was the last time a conversation over beer bong was about gay rights?

Brian: Yeah, and if I brought up LGBT issues in the middle of a frat party, I'd probably end up stuffed in the keg.

Rachel: (laughs)

Brian: But seriously, stuff like this happens every day. I have a friend who is totally in the closet, but gets along with his straight roommate really well. However, this roommate blasts Eminem songs that just send my friend further and further into the closet. He probably has no idea that every time he sings along to these lyrics, he is basically talking about killing his gay roommate.

Rachel: Wow, that's horrible. Freshman housing situations can be pretty crazy, especially with randomly assigned homophobic roommates. So how's dorm life treating you?

Brian: It's going great, actually. Before filling out my housing application, I had already found a roommate who would be accepting of me, so we chose to live together. I just didn't want to feel the need to hide my sexuality or deal with someone feeling uncomfortable because of it. But as it turns out, I have to deal with that anyway. Even though I am fortunate to be on a floor with LGBT allies, there have definitely been those uncomfortable moments. For example, a couple times this year, I have been brushing my teeth in the bathroom, when the door would open and a guy would start to walk in to go take a shower, but then take one look at me and turn around and leave. I think it's really bizarre that other people would be that uncomfortable with me just brushing my teeth while they are taking a shower. It's not like I'm going to bust through the shower curtain to watch them. They're not that hot anyway!

Rachel: (laughs)

Brian: But really, having something like that happen right before a class not only takes your mind out of the classroom, but kind of consumes it for the whole day. Of course, all students come to

61

class with other issues and baggage, but for many LGBT students, these issues are always there and impossible to ignore.

RACHEL: Yeah, and so often they're completely invisible, too.

BRIAN: So, have you heard from anyone else who is upset by the hate crime?

RACHEL: Everyone I've talked to who has heard about it has been really disturbed, except a few people who told me they didn't believe it was a hate crime because it's not that unusual for a drunk college boy to yell "faggot" and "throw some punches," which I find really disturbing. The problem is really all of the people who have no idea what's going on. If you miss one D.O. article, you're completely clueless to this. But, on the plus side, those who do know about it seem to be very concerned and even more supportive of the LGBT community than they were before. But, I guess it's easier to support the LGBT community when they are victims.

BRIAN: Yeah, that's an interesting point. It's a shame that it takes something like this to bring people together and support one another. It's too bad the bystanders and everyone watching while it happened couldn't rally together and speak up then. Everyone just watched it happen like it was some kind of show.

RACHEL: Wait, were you there?

BRIAN: Okay, I guess you got me. Not only was I there, but the victim who was attacked that night was my friend. I was there and saw everything happen right in front of me. After calling me and my friends faggots, the attacker threw my friend to the ground and went at him with everything he had. He kept saying things to him like, "I'm going to kill you." The attacker just kept punching him in the head and beating him, even while we were on our cell phones with 911. I could barely even stand up when this was happening. My stomach turned into a knot and I just froze. Worst of all, the guy just wouldn't stop. My friend would get away for a couple of seconds, but then the attacker just came back after him and beat him harder than before. At one point he was slamming him into the pavement and I also remember his head being smashed into the hood of a car.

RACHEL: Damn. Is he okay? Are you okay?

BRIAN: Yeah. He's doing okay now. The skin was all scraped off of his arms and elbows and I felt some blood around the back of his head. But he insisted that he was going to be okay and he just wanted to get some rest. As for me, now I sometimes think twice about whether or not it's safe to go outside. I sometimes find myself looking around at other people, wondering if they would hate, or even hurt, me if they knew I was gay. It's been especially hard dealing with my classes because I have so much to deal with outside of them. Every time I come back to my room I have a message from someone who wants to talk to me. It's especially difficult because I am going through so much on my own and this is taking a lot out of me. I mean, this is only my second week of college. I don't even know who my friends are or where I fit in yet. I feel like this is distorting that whole process. It sucks that sometimes I'll just get done telling the story to someone who needs to know it, and then I have to wipe my tears and put on a happy face and go to class where it feels like none of this stuff even matters.

RACHEL: I don't know how you'd even have time to think about classes. Do your professors know about this?

BRIAN: Well, I sent an email to all of my professors. I only heard back from two of them, and they were both very supportive. My women's studies professor and TA were very understanding. They came to me and said that the women's studies office was a safe space that I could come to any time, even if it's just to study or whatever. They also said not to worry about it if I got behind in reading and class work for a little bit. That really helped to make me feel much less stressed out.

RACHEL: So... where does all this leave you?

BRIAN: Well, obviously it hurt a lot. I kind of lost faith in people when everyone just stood around. We even talked to two witnesses afterwards who knew the attacker, but they never came forward. So, no one has been charged with the attack.

RACHEL: Great. So thanks to them, either one of us could be sitting in a class next to somebody who might want to kill us?

BRIAN: Yeah . . . kind of sucks, doesn't it? I guess we just have to focus on the good that's coming out of this. I mean, people are coming together to speak out, and even if it did take something like this for it to happen, at least it's happening. I think we could really make some good out of a bad situation. This has really motivated me to get more involved in LGBT and diversity activism, even if it's just speaking up in the classroom.

IN THE CLOSET

>>>referred to by LGBT people as the state of hiding one's LGBT-identity from others, and, sometimes, oneself

RACHEL: It's really cool that you're willing to do that. But at the same time, it sucks how the entire burden of making the classroom a safe space can fall on the shoulders of queer students. I would think that a classroom that feels like a safe space would be a more comfortable environment for everybody. I don't know whether my TAs and professors are scared of dealing with this stuff or if they just have the privilege of not thinking about it.

BRIAN: Yeah. If they only understood how their silence echoes across campus.

The Importance of LGBT Allies

Camille Baker

What is an ally? Webster's dictionary defines an ally as "one that is associated with another as a helper." However, this definition is broad. A person can be an ally to a community service organization, a political organization, or a certain group of individuals such as lesbian, gay, bisexual and transgendered (LGBT) students. An ally can lend a helping hand in an assortment of ways through actions and words. There are people everywhere who are allies to many different groups and individuals and Syracuse University is no different. After interviewing several students who consider themselves to be allies of the LGBT community, I found there are different ways of being allies, and these variations seem to exist along a continuum that ranges from being a "potential ally" to an "active ally." Allies exist at either extreme, but more often than not allies find themselves situated somewhere in between.

If I had to pick a potential ally out in a crowd, it would be nearly impossible, which is why it is important to talk about this type of ally. A potential ally might not let you know he or she is an ally, preferring to be anonymous. If someone says something derogatory or discriminating against a LGBT person, the anonymous ally may not respond, but he or she will think it's wrong. Most of the time, these allies will share their opinions only when in the company of friends or others with whom they feel comfortable. Potential allies often lack the confidence or encouragement to become more active allies. However, potential allies can become more visibly engaged if they are encouraged to speak their minds. This is why creating a classroom environment in which homophobia and heterosexism are challenged is so important; when potential allies know that their opinions are respected and supported, they will be more likely to allow their position to be heard.

Allies who find themselves in between the potential and active ally roles are a little more recognizable because they are often comfortable enough to display their ally status through voicing their opinions, using the "Safe Space" stickers, or participating in LGBT-related campus events. A sophomore biomedical physics major told me that she lets people know her position on LGBT issues whenever these discussions arise. She does not go out of her way to make sure people know she is an ally, but she does speak out publicly when necessary. For example, she told me, "If I ever hear someone call another student a 'faggot' or say that something is 'gay' I call him or her on it," she said. "That type of language just keeps the stereotypes alive." While these students may be willing to challenge homophobic comments and the ideologies behind them in the classroom, they need instructors and TAs to foster an environment that allows these discussions to take place.

At the far end of the ally continuum is the active ally. These allies are fewer in numbers, but are important in supporting LGBT students throughout the campus. The active ally is present at most LGBT-sponsored events and even helps coordinate

ALLY

>>>a person who works in a helpful capacity toward another; supports and honors sexual and gender diversity, etc.

them. It is easy to spot active allies because they aggressively promote their LGBT-supportive position. For example, in debates about LGBT issues, such as legalizing same-sex marriage, an active ally would speak out openly, but would also contact his or her senators, write a letter to the *Syracuse University Daily Orange* or even organize campus events to raise awareness of the issues. An active ally is not afraid to speak out in support of LGBT people regardless of the situation.

It is important to know that due to widespread homophobia and heterosexiam, being a LGBT ally is not easy. Allies of LGBT students are at risk of the same discrimination and hostility that members of the LGBT community face daily, often because a LGBT ally's sexuality is always put into question once it is known that the person is an ally. More disturbing, allies, as well as LGBT students, can face threats of violence. I suspect that this might be why there are more potential allies than active allies.

Allies in the Classroom

As a Black and Mexican female I understand what it is like to be marginalized in the classroom. Discussions that involve race and ethnicity often leave me feeling alienated, not because I am different from my peers, but because I am frequently the only person of color in the classroom. In these types of situations I feel that I need to speak for all people of color, when really that is not possible. When I find myself in this position I look for students who are my allies, which (depending on the level and visibility of their activism) may be either an easy task or a difficult one. While my racial and ethnic status is easily identifiable, a person's marginalized status based on his or her sexuality or gender identity may not be as easily seen. But, every classroom in all disciplines has LGBT students and their allies who would like to broaden the understanding of diversity from the simplified black/white issue that it has been considered on this campus. Instead, we recognize the range of identities, behaviors, cultures, and abilities that exist on our campus and we work to incorporate these various forms of difference in our

A major <problem> LGBT student allies face is lack of awareness.

classroom discussions of diversity. However, we need help in this endeavor from our instructors and TAs.

It was not until my second year living in residence halls that I began to encounter students who openly identified as LGBT. Since then I have found it hard to ignore the ever-present issues surrounding LGBT students on the Syracuse University campus. After knowing my new LGBT friends for no more than a month, I was forced to confront homophobia when two of them were victims of a hate-crime based on their sexuality. While this situation was worthy enough to gain front-page status in *The Daily Orange* and sparked a fire within the LGBT community to raise awareness, as allies, my friends and I were frustrated that it failed to take precedence in our classrooms. To my surprise, a course that focused on current events did not even mention this hate crime in the days and weeks following the incident. In addition, it was not until a week after the incident that the issue was finally discussed in my sociology class.

From my ally perspective, the problem with situations like this is the silence that pervades academic spaces when dialogue provoking awareness and encouraging respect should occur. Professors and teaching assistants are in a position to bring about that change. First, professors and teaching assistants need to recognize

VOICES

I think a lot of (straight) people are reluctant to support (LGBT people) because people will think they're gay.

>SU undergraduate student

that diversity is incorporated into *all* aspects of life and areas of study and is therefore relevant to all disciplines. While many students understand that not everyone is going to have the same morals or values, for the students who do not understand this it is even more important to provide discussions that expose them to ideologies that differ from their own. As a person in an authoritative position, a professor or teaching assistant can act as an ally and bring the topic of diversity on campus, including a focus on LGBT issues, into the spotlight.

A major problem LGBT student allies face is lack of awareness. If professors or teaching assistants took the time to mention LGBT campus events before lecture begins, students might begin to understand that SU's LGBT-community is vibrant, active, and supported by many allies, including faculty, throughout campus. Increasing student awareness of the LGBT and other marginalized campus communities shows that professors and teaching assistants care about all of their students. Professors and teaching assistants can improve the discussion of LGBT issues on campus by bringing up these topics in English, engineering, anthropology, public relations, advertising, the sciences, management, and all the other areas of study available on the Syracuse University campus.

When professors and teaching assistants work as allies to know more about LGBT issues on campus, they can then create classroom environments that allow for a richer discussion of diversity. If professors conceptualize sexuality and gender as an integral part of recognizing the diversity in their curriculum and classroom spaces, SU could create a more inclusive educational environment that

benefits all students. The main course of action a professor or teaching assistant should take is to show they are allies to the LGBT community by allowing their students to engage with these dialogues. However, through my discussions with student allies on campus, I learned that it is important that a professor or teaching assistant not police the discussion, but facilitate it. When the LGBT hate crime was briefly mentioned in one of her classes, a sophomore advertising major who I talked with did not know what to say. "My parents always tried to expose me to new ideas and cultures when I was growing up, so it is not hard for me to openly discuss different ideas and opinions," she explained. But, when the LGBT hate crime was briefly mentioned in one of her communications courses, she was uncomfortable because the space for her ideas seemed too controlled by the professor. "I wanted to discuss the topic more," she said, "but my professor kind of moved the conversation into a different direction before I could get my opinion out there." If the professor had spent more time on the issue or allowed students to discuss it more, then maybe she wouldn't have been so "uncomfortable" and would have been able to voice her thoughts, making her ally status more visible and inspiring other students to do the same.

If LGBT issues continue to be ignored in classrooms, no good can come from incidents like the hate crime mentioned earlier. The potential for the active participation of all levels of allies in classrooms across campus is high. A professor's or teaching assistant's role in the classroom is to expose students to new and different ideas. The student's role is to take advantage of such exposure, continue to grow, and become a responsible member of society. By incorporating LGBT issues into areas of study that do not normally address these topic, or by engaging students in conversations about the richness of campus diversity, professors and TAs help students gain a greater awareness of the world in which they live and this is likely to encourage them to actively identify as allies, thus promoting future dialogue and activism. These students will leave Syracuse University knowing that their ally identities were developed and supported while participating in classroom spaces that truly value diversity.

>>REFERENCES

"Ally." *Merriam-Webster's collegiate dictionary tenth edition.* (1997). Springfield, MA: Merriam-Webster, Incorporated.

Queer TAs in the Classroom:

Perspectives on Coming Out

Eldar Beiseitov and Payal Banerjee

Introduction

This essay addresses how LGBT graduate students, teaching assistants, and professors feel about discussing their sexual identities in the classroom, and the implications of being out in the classroom. Our essay is informed by a series of informal discussions with LGBT and non-LGBT teaching assistants on campus. These conversations have provided us with a range of opinions and concerns about this topic. Here we present and analyze some of these insights by juxtaposing the fears and concerns about personal disclosure in the classroom with arguments for this disclosure.

Personal Disclosure and the Teaching Process

One of the arguments against the disclosure of one's identity in the classroom is that the instructor has to maintain a degree of professionalism and formality when working with students. Revealing information about one's personal life or sexual/gender identity may be considered a detriment to creating a positive learning environment. For example, students who are uncomfortable with LGBT issues may feel insecure about voicing their opinions in the class; students with strong oppositions may aggressively express their views and interfere with the learning and teaching process; students who do not identify as LGBT may believe that the instructor favors queer students and their allies.

Despite these concerns, we would like to suggest that our readers consider challenging these notions. At the fundamental level there exists an indefinite number of issues, other than sexuality, that may potentially threaten students' comfort zones. Concealing one's identity in an attempt to avoid controversy creates a sterile and over-protective classroom. A significant proportion of these fears can be mitigated by solid teaching methods: for example, creating an atmosphere of healthy discussions, or assigning short reflection papers and group projects that can make students confidant in expressing their personal opinions without feeling threatened or silenced. Well explained and explicit grading and participation policies would ensure fairness for all students, thereby reducing concerns about any type of favoritism.

Hard Science and Coming Out

A second argument against disclosure is that the subject of sexuality may not be relevant to the content of the course. For example, in physics or mathematics the instructor's sexual identity should not matter and adds no useful context for learning the material. While the issue of sexuality or identity may be relevant in the humanities or the social sciences, it may not only be inconsequential, but also questionable, in other fields. Our position on this concern is that the classroom is not merely about course content but is also a social environment influenced and shaped by personal interactions. How we learn and how much we learn is often determined by these exchanges regardless of the subject matter. Examples or anecdotes used to illustrate and animate what appear to be objective scientific concepts often rely on

xpressions

COMING OUT

>>>process of disclosing one's LGBT identity and/or behavior; can be a lifelong process of self-acceptance

heterosexism and other dimensions of social inequality as demonstrated elsewhere in this book.[1] Furthermore, countless professors and TAs casually speak about what they did with their wife/husband, children, or family during vacations or holidays in the classroom, regardless of the discipline, and this self-expression about family and personal affection is seldom questioned as being unprofessional, distracting, or irrelevant.

The classroom is a microcosm of everyday social life and intersects with all the other things we are, and do, outside of it. In this context, we must remember that students have LGBT family members, friends, allies, and colleagues, and many are themselves LGBT. In this regard, it seems pointless and exclusionary for instructors to maintain heteronormative decorum in the classroom.

Political Agenda

Another argument against discussing sexual identities in classrooms is that instructors' openness about their identities may be interpreted by students as a political statement. The classroom, according to this position, should not be used as a forum for pushing an LGBT agenda.

As previously discussed, reservations against using classroom space and time for LGBT issues frames sexual identity as

being isolated from, and unrelated to, other critical topics of social significance that are commonly and openly discussed in class such as: women's invisibility in mathematics and the sciences, western canonization in art and literature, and so on. Moreover, the classroom does not exist in a vacuum nor is it socially neutral. The classroom is prefigured as a space determined by race relations, gender, (dis)ability, and class relations (who gets to attend college or which people are more likely to earn Ph.D.s and become professors), and as such it is already a political space. In this context, viewing openness about LGBT identities as an imposed political statement serves to "other" queerness and indicates unawareness of these issues.

LGBT instructors
can and should
serve us as **\<positive\>**
role models for
both
heterosexual and queer students

73

Instructors preoccupied with concerns about concealing their LGBT identity spend an inordinate amount of mental energies preserving the impression of assumed heterosexuality. These inhibitions can obstruct the fluency and joy of teaching. In contrast, openness about one's sexuality can enhance teaching and learning. It is important for LGBT instructors to be "whole" persons in all walks of life: trying to cover this very important aspect of people's lives, specifically if they do not wish to, is not only unhealthy and repressive but also perpetuates heteronormativity. LGBT instructors can and should serve us as positive role models for both heterosexual and queer students.

Concluding Remarks

As humans, we are many things at the same time and many of our markers are out in the open. For example, in most cases, we embody and carry our racial and ethnic backgrounds. We are perceived as either

Voices

A TA should try to de-dramatize the process of coming out in order to avoid silencing certain opinions. I did it in passing, in a non-threatening, non-aggressive way.

>Teaching Assistant

biological males or females. Our diverse accents, languages, religions, ages, (dis)abilities, or national identities may also be obvious from our words, actions, clothing, names, rituals, and celebrations. The rights or privileges we may or may not have, or the documents we carry on us as "proof" of the legitimacy of our presence in the U.S., simultaneously speak to the multiple identifiers of our backgrounds and social locations. Given these conditions, why must special care be exercised to shroud instructors' sexual or gender identity?

>>linked>>>>>>>>>>>>>>>>>>>>>>>>>>>>>

CLAGS >> web.gc.cuny.edu/clags/online.htm

CLAGS (Center for Lesbian and Gay Studies) contains a wide range of information for any academic interested in scholarly LGBT content.

Should we consciously hide our racial backgrounds or other markers in an effort to be professional or effective teachers in the classroom? Do we question whether being a woman, a black TA, or a young or old person will "distract" students from understanding the concepts in molecular biology or subatomic particles? In SU's current efforts to create a more diverse and comfortable learning and teaching environment, it is unconscionable to challenge the ability of any teacher to teach effectively based on her or his identity, including sexual or gender identity, sex, race, (dis)ability, age, social class, religion, and/or culture.[2]

>>ENDNOTES

1 > See Susan Adams or Ahoura Afshar, both in this volume, for examples.

2 > We would like to emphasize that graduate students, TAs, and instructors reserve the right to decide whether or not to disclose their sexual identity. The decision to do so is individual and must be respected as such.

ENGAGING
nuances

Understanding Current LGBT-Related Policies and Debates

Nicole Dimetman

Although it sometimes feels like it, Syracuse University does not exist in a vacuum. Instead, students here are simultaneously engaged with our campus culture as well as the larger society in which we live. The following discussions contextualize the experiences of LGBT students in light of current policies and debates that focus on the lives of lesbians, gay men, bisexual, and transgender people in the contemporary United States. While the topics here do not fully address the range of issues that LGBT people must constantly negotiate, they serve as a starting point for those who are unfamiliar with current legislation and controversy to begin to engage with subjects that concern many of us. Readers are encouraged to continue exploring the current relationship between the LGBT community and the primary social institutions of our culture by following the internet links provided at the end of the article. Please note: while the following information, facts and statistics were current in 2004, our culture is ever-changing, and rights legislation is both supportive of and detrimental to the experiences of people in LGBT communities.

Legislating Sex

Until 2003, many states outlawed any "unnatural" (non-procreative) sexual conduct, defined as sodomy. Although many heterosexuals engage in various kinds of non-procreative sex, homosexuals were disproportionately affected by enforcement practices. Under these laws, LGBT citizens, found in the privacy of their own homes having sex, were subject to arrest, prosecution, and/or fines. Those convicted under sodomy laws were also potentially labeled "sex offenders" by the State for the rest of their lives, a particularly degrading and debilitating consequence in the face of widespread sex offender websites and employee background checks. However, in 2003, the Supreme Court of the United States recognized a compelling argument in the case of *Lawrence v. Texas* and, in a 5-4 decision, the court ruled that state laws criminalizing sodomy were an unconstitutional invasion of privacy. This landmark decision effectively invalidated all contrary state laws and insured that homosexuals would never again be *legally* persecuted for their sexual practices.

Xpressions

SEXUAL ORIENTATION

>>>favored term to refer to an individual's emotional, sexual, and/ or romantic attractions to the same and/or opposite sex/gender

Gay Adoption

Although there were problems with reporting because people could not identify as gay on the response form, the 2000 Census counted approximately 600,000 same-sex couples. Some estimates suggest there are between 6 and 14 million children with at least one gay parent. Although many homosexuals have children from prior heterosexual relationships, gays and lesbians are seeking to adopt in ever-greater numbers.

While only three states (Florida, Mississippi, and Utah) have laws that explicitly prohibit same-sex adoption, according to the Human Rights Council (HRC), courts in 10 states tend to discriminate against same-sex couples wishing to adopt. Furthermore, only six states (Connecticut, Illinois, Massachusetts,

New Jersey, New York, and Vermont) and the District of Columbia have made second-parent adoption available statewide. This provides the equivalent of step-parent adoptions to gay and lesbian couples.

The Right to Serve

In 1992, President Clinton signed "Don't Ask, Don't Tell, Don't Pursue." Under the policy, military commanders are prohibited from inquiring about an officer's sexual orientation. The "Don't Tell" policy allows for the investigation and administrative discharge of service members if they either make a statement indicating that they are lesbian, gay or bisexual, engage in physical contact with someone of the same sex for the purposes of sexual gratification, or marry (or attempt to marry) someone of the same sex. The "Don't Pursue" policy bars anti-gay harassment as well as homosexual purges and certain other invasive investigations that have been used over the years to root out gay, lesbian, and bisexual service members. However, policy and practice are often two different things.

Unfortunately, women and young adults ages 18 to 25 are disproportionately affected by this policy, according to the Servicemembers Legal Defense Network (SLDN). Overall, the SLDN reports that women made up 15% of the armed forces in 2002, but accounted for 31% of those discharged under the law. Women are investigated often in retaliation for poor performance reviews, after refusing a man's sexual advances, or after reporting a man for sexual harassment. The 2002 Defense Department inspector general survey also found a "substantial" difference in responses according to level of service, which typically corresponds with the age of the service member. For example, 78% of respondents stated that enlisted service members were harassed in violation of "Don't Ask, Don't Tell." Only 2% said the same for officers. Since its passage, more than 9,000 persons suspected of being homosexual by their superiors have been discharged from military service at a cost of over a quarter of a billion tax dollars.

Gays in the Workplace

Currently, there is no federal law preventing workplace discrimination on the basis of sexual orientation. Only 14 states and the District of Columbia have laws banning sexual orientation employment discrimination in the public and private sectors. An additional 11 states have similar laws that are effective only in the public sector. This means that in most states people fired because they are a part of a sexual minority have no sure legal remedy. The Employment Non-

Discrimination Act (ENDA), H.R. 2692, was introduced in the House of Representatives and the Senate on July 31, 2001 with significant bipartisan support, but the Senate continues to deliberate the bill. The Human Rights Council reports 7,210 workplaces offering domestic partner benefits, an affirmative statement of non-discrimination. Further, 2,579 companies, including Syracuse University, have non-discrimination policies that include sexual orientation, but these policies are optional, at best.

Transgender Rights

In 2004, four states (California, Minnesota, New Mexico, and Rhode Island), 10 counties, and 55 cities included gender identity and expression under their anti-discrimination laws. Clearly, this represents a very small portion of local and state-wide anti-discrimination statutes. Under these laws, transgender individuals are usually protected from discrimination in housing and employment, but these statutes are not consistent and only occasionally cover the domain of public accommodations and are even less likely to ensure protection from discrimination in public education systems. In fact, of the four states that include some protection for transgender people, only Minnesota guarantees them a right against discriminatory policies and practices at

public schools. Although many regions continue to add transgender-inclusive legislation, this is clearly an area where laws do not match their necessity: transgender people often report that biased treatment and violence are frequently directed toward them due to their non-normative gender identities.

Civil Unions, Domestic Partnerships, and Gay Marriage

Though not always apparent, there are many differences between civil unions, domestic partnerships, and marriage.

Same-sex marriage is the only status that confers all the benefits of heterosexual marriage, including all those previously discussed.

Civil unions, available only in Vermont and only to same-sex couples, provide the same *state* benefits received by married persons in the state, but these unions are not recognized outside the state of Vermont (except in California and Massachusetts).

Domestic partnerships are available through some states, namely California, and are also offered by private and public sector employers for the purpose of extending employer related benefits to same-sex partners. However, domestic partnerships are not recognized by most states, or by the U.S. government. Importantly, many people within and beyond the LGBT community feel that marriage is the only choice towards full equality for LGBT partners. Civil unions and domestic partnership create a separate, but unequal, system: one that history has proven unconstitutional.

Is Marriage a Right?

The issue of whether same-sex partners should have access to legally recognized marriages is contentious at best. A December 2003 bipartisan poll conducted jointly by Public Opinion Strategies and Greenberg Quinlan Rosner Research shows that only 30% of likely voters favored allowing same-sex couples the right to marry, 56% opposed such legislation, and 13% were undecided. A similar poll asking about civil unions showed 42% in favor, 49% opposed, and 8% undecided. These numbers show high levels of opposition to gay marriage, but despite this widespread disapproval, the Massachusetts Supreme Court has recently ruled that laws barring gay couples from marriage are discriminatory and has asked its legislature to begin issuing marriage licenses to gay couples.

Arguments supporting gay marriage indicate the many benefits denied to committed gay couples that are enjoyed by their heterosexual counterparts. According to a 1997 Government Accounting Office (GAO) report, the federal government denies 1,049 benefits to same-sex couples because either they are not allowed to marry or their unions are not legally recognized as the equivalent. More specifically, here are some examples of benefits that are systematically denied to members of the LGBT community:

> As unmarried partners, gays and lesbians are unable to receive Social Security survivor benefits which translate into an average loss of $166,000 for a life expectancy of 77. Because many gay and lesbian

...rights legislation is both

SUPPORTIVE of

and

DETRIMENTAL to

the <experiences> of people in LGBT communities.

partners are also legally denied the opportunity of second-parent adoption, the loss of income is compounded since a shared child is additionally denied survivor benefits of up to $900 per month.

>
> Federally recognized marriages enjoy many tax exemptions that same-sex couples do not have access to, such as the estate and gift tax exemption, which allows property to be transferred, without tax penalty, from one spouse to another.

>
> Current immigration laws deny gays and lesbians the right to petition the government for the residency or citizenship of their same sex partners.

>
> The Federal Family and Medical Leave Act allowing married spouses up to 12 weeks of unpaid leave to take care of a seriously ill partner, parent, or child does not extend to same-sex couples.

As the polls show, views on same sex marriage are highly polarized. The Family Research Council illustrates the arguments against gay marriage and civil unions by highlighting two principles. The first is that marriage should not, and cannot, be extended to same-sex couples because it is a construct that precedes the U.S. Constitution. Marriage, they argue, is the recognition of a social reality whereby two adults, capable of natural reproduction, form a committed relationship toward the bearing and rearing of children. Thus, in the opinion of these opponents, marriage is necessary for the survival of society and should be protected from the government since it, in turn, benefits the larger culture. Because homosexuals cannot engage in a relationship that biologically produces a child, they should not reap the same rewards as those members of society who can. The second argument posed by the Family Research Council is that homosexual relationships are harmful to their participants. Proponents of this position argue that extending marriage privileges to homosexuals would confer a stamp of approval on a harmful lifestyle and would further deteriorate the importance of the family in America.

Fearing the eventual extension of marriage to same-sex couples, conservative groups have organized campaigns nationally, and in every state, by lobbying for the passage of Defense of Marriage Acts (DoMAs). However, supporters of these proposals are not limited to groups with clear anti-gay intentions. Instead, in 1996, President Bill Clinton, often considered the most LGBT-supportive president, signed a *national* DoMA that declared any civil union, domestic partnership, or same-sex marriage need not be acknowledged outside the state in which it was established. Since its passage, many states have passed their own DoMA laws codifying this idea in their state legislature. However, still unsatisfied with local and state-level DoMAs, President Bush has recently asked the U.S. Congress to add an amendment to the U.S. Constitution declaring marriage as a legal union exclusively between a man and a woman.

This amendment would prevent all states from adopting future laws that would counter this definition.

No doubt, this issue will continue to be a hot button between conservative groups and gay rights advocates for years to come.

Nature v. Nurture

Ah, the eternal debate: are gay people born that way or do they choose to be gay? Many gay men and lesbians say they've known they were attracted toward members of their own gender since they were very young. Explaining that a "choice" was never posed, or made, these stories serve the argument that there must be a genetic cause to sexual orientation. In fact, throughout the last few decades, many gay rights activists hoped that the discovery of a biological basis for homosexuality would lead them to winning legal rights for the

VOICES

Fear of being discovered can prevent an instructor from asserting a certain position. This is especially damaging in a social science classroom.

>Teaching Assistant

LGBT community. The thinking here is that if sexual orientation were immutable, then people in the LGBT community deserve protection from discrimination, similar to other "minority groups" such as people of color and people with disabilities. However, biological studies into a "gay gene" have been inconclusive at best, leading many critics of this type of research to ask, "instead of looking for a gay gene maybe it would be easier to find a straight gene?" a challenge which, not surprisingly, has gone unmet. Instead, a biological basis for sexual orientation remains undiscovered.

Social scientists continue to contribute to the Nature v. Nurture debate by arguing that human behaviors are always social and historical, not innate or biologically determined. In this perspective, every society creates its own set of sexual rules, meanings, discourses, and practices and people engage in these social systems according to the options that are made available to them through their culture and historical time period. This Social Constructionist perspective sees the categories of "homosexual" and "heterosexual" as inherently social—created by people—and cites historical literature to support the fact that these ways of understanding sexual life is a distinctly modern, and western, phenomenon.

An extension of the Social Constructionist paradigm, known as Queer Theory, further argues that the construction of these labels (homosexual, heterosexual, bisexual) serves to shape the way people experience their own desires. In other words, Queer Theory sees sexual statuses as "a language that frames what we know as bodies, desires, sexualities, identities" and that these systems of meanings influence us to understand our seemingly "innate" sexuality in terms of socially created categories (Seidman, 1996, p. 12). No matter what the "cause" of same-sex desires, we know that we make meaning of these differences in relation to the society in which we live. It is through these shared understandings that differences form hierarchies of privilege—privileges that, as shown throughout this article, are not rewarded equally between the LGBT community and those who identify as heterosexual. Nonetheless, the bottom line when it comes to the Nature v. Nurture debate is: why does it matter?

>>linked>>>>>>>>>>>>>>>

NGLTF >> www.thetaskforce.org

NGLTF (National Gay and Lesbian Task Force) is a national progressive organization working for the civil rights of LGBT people.

>>The author would like to thank Kathleen Farrell for her substantial contributions to this essay.

>>REFERENCES

Seidman, S. (1996). Introduction. In S. Seidman (Ed.), *Queer theory/sociology* (pp. 1-29). Malden, MA: Blackwell.

(Trans)Gendering the Classroom

Rob S. Pusch

I've spent a large part of my life studying gender. I don't mean only academic study, although I have done that, but I've analyzed it as part of my every day life. As a person who identifies as transgender, I am in a position to think about gender differently than those who never question their gender or only consider it unconsciously. In this essay I first look at what it means to be gendered, then I explore the meaning of *transgender* and talk about the experiences of being transgender in the classroom.

Being Gendered

Gender is a means of organizing social experiences, of understanding how individuals are expected to interact within society and to construct their lives. Gender is one of the first determinations we make about a person: "Is it a boy or a girl?" is almost always the first question asked when a child is born. Within American culture, people assume there are only two gender categories, man/boy and woman/girl. It is assumed that gender is synonymous with one's assigned birth sex:

those considered male are boys who will grow into men, and those considered female are girls who will grow into women. Sex and gender assignment is initially based on the appearance of genitalia.[1] From the moment infants are sexed, and gendered, they begin to be socialized in particular ways that encourage them to publicly present themselves as the gender that coincides with their identified birth sex. In the United States this begins in simple ways, such as "pink is for girls" and "blue is for boys." The development of gender is accompanied by assumptions about how a person interacts with others, how one behaves, and the roles one will take on, such as parenting and occupational roles. Gender is also demonstrated through the use of clothing, hair, mannerisms, voice, and other gendered actions. These are the foundations for learning how to create ourselves as appropriately gendered persons so others can perceive us as fitting into the correct gender category.

Social conventions for gendered roles and presentation are reinforced within everyday life through social institutions such as families, schools, the classroom, and the mass media. It is through these institutions that gender is reproduced and can be seen as socially constructed. This then feeds into how we, as agents within our culture, construct our seemingly personal identities as men or women. Despite this understanding of the socially constructed nature of gender, there is still the fundamental assumption that gender is only performed upon appropriately sexed bodies. What happens, then, when someone breaks this rule?

Xexpressions

GENDER IDENTITY

>>>one's personal sense of being a man or woman; the name one uses to refer to his/ her gender

Breaking Gender Rules

Growing up as a masculine female, I was often confronted in women's restrooms by comments such as "you're in the wrong restroom; this is the women's room!" I would exclaim that I was in the right place, but was left feeling I had done something wrong. From a young age I was breaking the rules of gender because I was a girl with short hair who wore masculine clothing. For gender outlaws, these transgressions are often met with confusion, anxiety, or hostility from the people around us. Even though our

88

genitals and other secondary sex characteristics may not be visible for public viewing, it is assumed that our gender presentation signifies the presence of particularly sexed bodies. Those who cannot be easily identified as a male or a female are typically blamed for causing others to be confused. These assumptions serve to maintain the rigid structure of the binary gender system by erasing the identities of those whose bodies and gender identities do not fit within the binary gender/sex construct. Those of us who identify as transgender disrupt these assumptions.

What is Transgender?

Public use of the term transgender has increased over the past five years. It is a broad term whose definition is still changing and does not define a single identity or behavior, but is generally defined as "someone who transcends the conventional definitions of 'man' and 'woman'. Butch lesbians, transsexuals, radical faeries, boss girls, crossdressers, drag queens, sissies, tomboys, and many other kinds of people vary from the conventional expectations of their birth gender" (American Boyz, 2001). The breadth of this definition encompasses a wide range of transgender people. This suggests that assumptions cannot be made about anyone who identifies as transgender. The stereotypical portrayal of a transgender person as "a man trapped in a woman's body," or vice versa, inaccurately describes the experience of many transgender people.

There are a variety of ways to conceptualize categories of gender. Many transgender persons do not feel comfortable in the gender assigned to them at birth but have varying degrees of identification with another gender category. Some transgender persons describe themselves as being third gendered. Some feel that there is a gender continuum. These other genders, populated by transgender persons, are not definable within the hegemonic binary gender system. They remind us that binary gender system is socially constructed and that the privileges accorded people based on gender are not natural and can be disrupted.

It is often difficult to explain this to those who have never questioned their own gender identity or cannot imagine anything beyond the binary gender system. For me, it's not that I feel like a particular gender, but rather I don't feel like the gender I was assigned at birth. I am not sure what it means to feel like a man, but I know I do not feel like woman. However, since others can only see two possible genders, my presentation as masculine marks me as a white middle class man, and often I am taken to be a gay man. Along with this comes a whole host of assumptions about who I am, how I should act in particular situations, and what my personal history and experiences have been. It also influences how others react and interact with me.

In the 10+ years since I first came out as transgender, I have seen a change in the visibility and representation of transgender persons. Ten years ago the term was rarely heard. The terms generally used were *transsexual* and *transvestite*, both of which came out of medical literature. Transsexual typically referred to people who felt they were born into the wrong body and desired to have their bodies changed through surgery to match their gender identities. Transvestite referred to those who dressed in the clothing of the opposite sex, or what is now commonly called crossdressing.

Over the past decade there have been an increasing number of mainstream articles on transgender persons. These include articles both about, and by, transgender persons, as well as the representation of transgender and transsexual persons in television and film. The representations of transgender persons have been mixed; some present transgender persons as transsexuals, individuals who feel they were born into the wrong body, or as persons who are merely misunderstood. Others portray transgender persons as the subjects of violence, including news media stories on transgender prostitutes who are murdered, and movies such as *Boys Don't Cry* (a movie about Brandon Teena), and *The Badge* (a movie about the murder of a transsexual sex worker). The common theme here is that the transgender people are murdered when their "deception" is discovered. The viewer is led to believe that the transgender individuals are responsible for their own murders because of the way they chose to live. Films like these help to construct shared understandings of what it means to be transgender in today's society and deeply influence adolescents who identify with, and relate to, these murder victims.

(Trans)Gender in the Classroom

How does being transgender impact campus, and more specifically, classroom experiences? For those who identify as transgender, a number of issues surface. Gender is a public display that is viewed by the people around us, thus the process of transition that many transgender people experience can be quite visible.[2] Those who successfully pass as a particular gender become invisible to those around them as transgender persons, but not all transitions go unnoticed. Being visible and invisible as transgender raises different issues on campus and in the classroom.

Transitioning on Campus

As mentioned previously, transition is a very public process, one that can be obvious to others. People who identify as transgender do not transition at the same rate, or in the same manner. Regardless, those who go through a time of being marked as breaking the unwritten rules of gender often cause anxiety and confusion among aquaintences and colleagues. This can result in many responses on campus and in the classroom.

For my dissertation (Pusch, 2003), I spoke with a number of transgender college students about their experiences of transition and the issues they faced. For example, one participant, Kristen,[3] spoke about her experience as an undergraduate

Voices

When teachers and students talk about the classroom as a safe space, I wonder-safe for whom?

>Beth Ferri (Teaching & Leadership & Cultural Foundations of Education)

student at a large private university. While she presented as a woman and had begun taking hormones, she had not yet legally changed her name. This meant that her school records were still in her "boy name." It is not uncommon for transgender students to be in this situation because going through the legal name change process can be costly and takes time. However, this meant that on campus she was typically called by Justin, not Kristen. One professor commented that he recognized her as a Smith, but that the name on his class list was Justin Smith and that couldn't be her. When she replied that it was, his response was "weird..." The professor was clearly confused by someone visually presenting as a woman, yet having a masculine name. While his feelings about the disjuncture between Kristen's presentation and her name on the class list are not uncommon, it succeeded in making Kristen feel uncomfortable identifying as transgender. The professor's reaction also shut down any potential discussion with Kristen about being transgender and how she preferred to be addressed in class.

Along with this discomfort of how to come out to faculty and explain to them how we wish to be addressed, transgender students often feel they end up having to educate others on what it means to be transgender. Often the burden is placed on us to become educators, or we are made to feel as if it is our responsibility to make others feel more comfortable around us. While some transgender people may not mind being put in the position of explaining what it means to be transgender, others see this as a burden. As one friend of mine commented, when he comes out to others, he ends up feeling like an object of curiosity—like a carnival exhibit, or a freak.

Gender is a <public> display **that is viewed by the people around us.**

Becoming Invisible

I've been on hormones for over five years and have, for the most part, become invisible as transgender. Since testosterone has successfully masculinized my appearance, people who do not know me, or who are meeting me for the first time, assume I am biologically male. Given the anxiety of the years when I was more obviously breaking the unwritten gender rules, you might imagine this is preferable. However, being invisible brings its own set of anxieties. Passing as male means that those who do not know I am transgender do not fully know me. While I may look male and appear to be a man, who I am is far more complex; who I am is also impacted by my personal history of being female and growing up as a girl.

Since transgender persons are at a greater risk of violence,[4] invisibility brings a measure of safety. This often leads transgender people to maintain their silence. As someone who is often invisible,

I am able to witness how oblivious others are to the presence of transgender persons and about how gender works in general. For example, last year I was observing a class in which students were responding to a talk on LGBT issues. One young woman summarized the talk saying "it was about lesbians, gays, bisexuals and ... what was that other thing?" Someone else had to say "transgender." While within the LGBT community many have at least heard about transgender persons, this young woman's comment was a reminder that not only do many people not understand transgender issues, they don't even know the word. This level of ignorance makes coming out in classrooms even more daunting.

While some of us are out about being transgender and try to educate others on transgender issues, many prefer the anonymity of passing. Within the classroom, faculty can, and should, work to create an environment that allows transgender students to feel safe no matter how they choose to present themselves. As more and more students begin to transition while in college, faculty will need to be aware of the steps they can take to help create an accepting environment. Faculty should be respectful of student requests such as using a name other than the one that appears on the class list, and using students' desired pronouns. Also, do not assume the student is openly transgender. While some students might come out to a faculty member, they may not be out to other students. Many students are concerned about the reactions of those around them as they go through the process of transitioning from one gender to another.[5]

>>References

American Boyz. (2001, March 3). Transgendered? The American Boyz. Retrieved January 15, 2004, from http://www.amboyz.org/articles/transgendered.html

Pusch, R. S. (2003). The bathroom and beyond: Transgendered college students' perspectives of transition (Doctoral dissertation, Syracuse University, 2003). *Dissertation Abstracts International, 64,* 456.

CONTINUED>>

>>Endnotes

1 > While there are individuals born intersexed, these genitals are assumed to be "abnormal" and are often surgically "corrected" as soon after birth as possible. For more information on intersexed persons see the website for the Intersexed Society of North America, http://www.isna.org

2 > *Transition* is a term used by transgender people to refer to the process of comingout and beginning to live as one's self-identified gender. This may or may not include medical intervention. Transition may also include changing one's name, pronoun use, and changing gender presentation. Medical interventions may include hormone therapy, some form of chest surgery, and/or genital alteration.

3 > Kristen is the pseudonym used for one of the participants in my dissertation research.

4 > Human Rights Campaign, in their Transgender Basics states "Transgender people are often targeted for hate violence based on their non-conformity with gender norms and/or their perceived sexual orientation. Hate crimes against transgender people tend to be particularly violent." For more information see http://www.hrc.org

5 > November 5th has been marked as the Day of Remembrance. For more information, as well as a list of names of transgendered persons who how been murdered see http://www.gender.org/remember/day/index.html

International Students and Sexuality at Syracuse University

Sidney Greenblatt

Syracuse University plays host to over 2,233 international students, scholars, and their dependents from 151 different countries and all geographic regions of the globe. While students from Asia are the visible, numerical majority, there have been demographic shifts in sub-regional and national representation: students from India are now the largest single national group on campus, displacing China and Taiwan in the past year. When teaching international students, it is important to recognize the many ways perspectives on and experiences with particular sexualities, races, ethnicities, abilities, nationalities, and religions intersect—just as it is important when teaching American students. These different perspectives, experiences, and levels of understanding sexuality shape the ways students make sense of LGBT issues in the classroom and on campus, more generally. Therefore, it is imperative that TAs begin to explore the variations that exist among their students.

Our international student population is

extremely diverse. Their American classmates, faculty, and staff are often poorly equipped to grasp differences among them. While there are exceptions, most Americans do not readily distinguish Muslims, Hindus, Sikhs, Jains, and Parsis or regional and local identities, languages and dialects. The assumption of homogeneity within these populations extends to students and scholars from nations other than India; few Americans speak or understand Cantonese, Taiwanese, Tibetan, Mongolian, or Fujian's multiple dialects. Nor do they recognize the differences between Han, Mongolians, Chinese Koreans, Hui, Bai, Yi, Manchus, and Tibetans, to name a few. These multiple nationalities, religions, and languages are just a few of the ways that Syracuse University has received its international reputation for diversity.

Despite all these variations, international students on campus are often described as people who represent "majorities" in their own countries. Conceptualizing international students as part of "majority" groups inhibits discussions of the differences that exist within these groups, including sexual and gender identity. While Americans acknowledge that gender is a form of diversity among international students, many may not understand the nuances in gendered identities that characterize internationals on campus. In fact, this is evident from the stereotypes that are often used to characterize international students.[1]

These generalizations frame any discussion of sexuality among international students. First, it is impossible to fathom attitudes and values about sexual identity, behavior, or gender expression without first recognizing the sources of diversity within the international student population. Second, understanding the diversity within our international student population reminds us that the context for any discussion of gender and sexuality has to be sufficiently nuanced to link sexual, religious, and socio/political experiences distinctly different from our own, and disconnect sexuality and attitudes about it from the Judeo-Christian legacy from which many Americans understand LGBT people and issues.

A substantial number of our international students and scholars come from patriarchal social systems pervaded by political ideologies and/or religious dogmas that result either in the censorship of information and activity related to sexuality in general, and non-heterosexuality in particular, or reiterate heterosexist norms as if they were the only acceptable standard for sexual, marital and social relationships. This would be familiar territory to Americans were it not for the fact that the religious and secular ideologies that frame sexual identities and behavior for most of our international students are Muslim, Confucian, Neo-Confucian, Hindu, secular socialist and communist, and not Judeo-Christian. In contemporary American society, it is possible to find safe space, even if it is limited, by escaping into the privatized sectors of secular society. However, in many of the countries from which our international students come, patriarchal control severely limits safe space and safe discourse.

In addition, our students, scholars, and their dependents also come from many societies suffering the ravages of civil war, terrorism, and internecine warfare, and some of them come from societies only recently in transition from conditions of conflict.[2] Governmental and heads of households alike all too often regard

VOICES

One of the things that I find is that I have no role-models. None. So, where are we supposed to find role models?

>SU undergraduate student

homosexuality as the manifestation not only of sexual deviance, but also of political dissonance. Those whose lives do not adhere to the acceptable social norms either retreat to very private spaces, self-censor, or flee. Politics, then, frames sexual identities and behaviors in more ways than those to which most Americans are accustomed.

To generalize is difficult, but the impact of these experiences often draws a deep line between what is private and what is public, leaving much less room for the expression of sexual and gender identity, particularly for women and transgender individuals. When political crisis is added to the ideological and religious mix, the room for expression is narrowed much further. Even when cultures are not experiencing such extreme turmoil, formal and informal laws, widespread belief systems, and cultural norms often work to silence, or severely stigmatize, those whose practices do not conform to that which is considered acceptable.

However, these larger social forces do not always effectively force LGBT people into invisibility. Instead, both historically and today, non-heterosexual identities are expressed throughout various cultures. When considering some Asian societies in particular, historical records attest to the fact that homosexual behavior was often practiced in the domains of the wealthy and powerful, in very private, familial spaces, and through the creation of special castes or statuses, primarily at the behest of the wealthy and the powerful. In China, for example, there is a long tradition of male homosexuality and, in many Indian societies, a Muslim caste-like organization of entertainers composed of homosexuals and transsexuals, known as Hijras, represent a little known identity (Ellingson & Green, 2002; Hinsch, 1990;

Nanda, 1990). When trying to make sense of how these ways of life became stigmatized, the literature on colonialism reminds us of the ways in which Western colonists described and portrayed the people they colonized and their institutions as either sexually depraved or sexually enticing, such as the sexual deviance attributed to harems and the zananas of the Middle East and India (Hunt & Lessard, 2002).

Rapid social change and globalization have broken the wall of silence that surrounds homosexuality and have begun to undermine the heterosexism of many nations around the globe, but not everywhere, or to equal degrees. Where international media reaches across the globe to touch the lives of individuals and families, more pluralities of attitude inform both exploration of sexual orientation and public expression of sexual and gender identities. Even in repressive societies, major metropolitan areas across the globe offer space for self-expression. Hong Kong, despite Chinese rule, offers more room than the mainland

SOCIAL CLASS

>>>usually refers to social stratum whose members share certain social, economic, and cultural characteristics

expressions

for expression of dissent in general. In South Korea, despite strong patriarchal structures, access to the internet and international media has created opportunities for people to connect with communities of people like them, encouraging greater levels of self-acceptance.

More specifically, in India, a democratic country undergoing very rapid change, homosexuality is now broached in new magazines, in television talk shows, novels, short stories on the internet, and in film. A protest movement now champions the cause of the Hijras and seeks justice and human rights protections for this marginalized group. Also, in China, the post Cultural Revolution era brought about a rebellion among college students who formed on-campus clubs exploring all aspects of sexual and gender identity. Now, one can find novels, films, magazines, graphic art, and rock music that impart stories of the influence of the Cultural Revolution on sexual identity. While fear persists among officials that these private practices and ideologies might yield public rebellion, media continue to offer a much more open approach to sexualities. Again, this growing inclusiveness of non-heterosexual identities is not occurring equally around the globe: in many nations, terrorism and civil strife continue to threaten groups deemed sexually and politically "deviant" and none of these countries accept non-heterosexual behaviors and identities as a suitable alternative to heterosexuality.

With this framework in mind, we can return to the experiences of international students in the context of Syracuse University. While they are mostly graduate students, many undergraduates also call another nation their home and both men and women from both levels of study tend to pursue degree programs predominantly in the sciences and engineering. These are not classroom cultures where sexuality is, itself, a subject of study and discussion, nor have most of our international students been in classrooms where it is. Heterosexism prevails, and that prevalence echoes most of these students' experiences at home. How, then, do international students who identify as other than heterosexual begin

Politics, then, frames sexual identities and behaviors in more ways than those to which most Americans are accustomed.

99

to feel supported, accepted, and respected for who they are?

Given the emphasis on "privacy" and concerns about "conventionality" that most international students are taught before coming to the U.S., the place to which most international students turn to explore all facets of sexuality is the internet. This exploration takes place, not in the classroom, but outside of it. However, there are clear efforts that TAs and faculty can make that can communicate a sense of support for their LGBT students from abroad. Perhaps a comment on a syllabus can indicate that all students are equally respected in a particular classroom, regardless of nationality, religion, gender identity, (dis)ability, or sexuality. You may also want to include contact information for the LGBT Resource Center on campus, along with the same information for the Slutzker Center for International Services. Placing a "SAFE SPACE" sticker on an office door symbolizes that those office residents respect LGBT students. Announcing campus events in classrooms, including events pertaining to non-heterosexual people and communities, is another way to indicate that you recognize and accept that your students come from a variety of social locations. And, when an occurrence on campus threatens the S.U. LGBT community, address these situations and make sure your students know where they can turn for support. These are all examples of how to communicate to your students that you understand how sexuality is an important component of your students' multiple identities, that you recognize how sexual identity and gender expression often shape students' experiences and social allegiances, and, most importantly, that you appreciate these differences.

It is critical to emphasize that international students who identify as non-heterosexual face a triple dilemma: first, they must deal with being international students in the United States, on a campus full of predominantly white and economically privileged students. Second, these international students must struggle with heteronormativity and homophobia in this country and among their fellow students on this campus; and third, they must also negotiate those same oppositional forces when in their home country. It takes very strong people to successfully embrace all of their identities under these circumstances. This is why it is so vital that our TAs and faculty members recognize their responsibility as allies to these populations and take that job very seriously.

>>REFERENCES

Ellingson, S. & Green, M.C. (Eds.). (2002). *Religion and sexuality in cross-cultural perspective*. New York: Routledge.

Hunt, T.L. & Lessard, M. (2002). *Women and the colonial gaze*. New York: NewYork Univesity Press.

Nanda, S. (1990). *Neither man nor woman: The hijras of India*. Belmont, CA: Wordsworth Publishing Company.

Wright, A. (1959). *Buddhism in Chinese history*. Stanford, CA: Stanford University Press.

>>ENDNOTES

1 > In the late 1970s and early 1980s, new arrivals from abroad were largely drawn from the top income earning families and selected from the best known educational institutions. That selectivity gave the appearance of homogeneity to the international student population on campus. But, from the mid-1980s onward, the international student population increased significantly and the recruitment base spread across regions, classes, linguistic, and ethnic groups fueling diversity within international student ranks. However, the notion that international students are homogeneous persists despite the changes in the composition of this population.

2 > Many of the countries that have either been in varying states of war and dissolution contribute small numbers to our international student population, but the significance of their experience looms large. They include students from Bolivia, Eritrea, Indonesia, Iran, Iraq, Israel, the Ivory Coast, Kosovo, Lebanon, Montenegro, Pakistan, Serbia, Tibet, and Zimbabwe.

Responsible Pedagogy

PART II

Constant Queerying:
Practicing Responsible Pedagogy at Syracuse University

Elizabeth Sierra-Zarella

Introduction

>> We need to make all members of this community, including TAs, aware that LGBT and queer people are members of this community and are in the classrooms whether visible or invisible, or whether they're wanting to be out that day or not. The first thing is making sure that everyone knows that the classrooms and those halls that we walk in, the staff that we talk to, our colleagues, are often members of LGBT practices and communities.
>>**>Jackie Orr (Sociology)**

When I was presented with the opportunity to author this chapter, I was both honored and humbled by the chance to make a lasting impression on the new cohort of teaching assistants. As a Ph.D. student in Child and Family Studies, I have just been appointed as a TA myself and am anxious to take my place in the classroom in the fall.

105

However, I realize that the university classroom can be a political minefield, especially in courses filled predominantly with first year students, many of whom have experienced privileged lifestyles before coming to Syracuse University and who may hold steadfast, unexamined beliefs about certain members of our diverse student population. Teaching through this barrier of misunderstanding and ignorance is a difficult task indeed. The conscientious instructor must not only teach through students' assumptions and misunderstandings, but also engage in a process of critical self-exploration of her own assumptions and beliefs. It is only through critical self-reflection that we can begin to understand our own limited frames of

Anything that doesn't problematize heteronormativity reinforces it.

>Claudia Klaver (English)

reference, and work to widen our understanding of and active support for a diverse range of students, staff, and colleagues. This book is intended as a starting point for instructors who are unfamiliar with LGBT issues and heteronormativity by demonstrating some pedagogical strategies used to address heteronormative assumptions and classroom practices.

This essay was compiled from 18 faculty and graduate student instructor interviews conducted by a team of volunteers dedicated to responsible teaching practices. The interviewees represent a wide range of academic disciplines and social locations and were selected based on their reputation for critical and inclusive pedagogy. Our collective hope is that these teachers' work will inspire you, the future professoriate, to acknowledge the reality of LGBT issues on campus and to help Syracuse University continue our mission of valuing diversity and continual personal growth through higher education. As Casey Sprock (College of Law) explains:

You can have your personal belief system, that's fantastic, [but] you are [also] going to respect the University culture that Syracuse wants to create, and that includes acknowledging that there might be LGBT students in your physics class. I understand that you're a high-energy physicist, that's great ... you just need to be aware that there will be students of different colors, and there will be women, and there will be people who have different abilities, and there will be people who are gay and lesbian in your classes.

Effectively acknowledging this entails recognizing and complicating heteronormative practices in your teaching methods. This essay in particular offers the opportunity for you, as a new TA, to hear from SU faculty who offer advice, suggestions, and examples of dynamic practices for a responsible LGBT pedagogy.

What is LGBT Pedagogy anyway?

There is no one theory of LGBT pedagogy. In fact, many faculty respondents used different terms such as LGBT, Queer, and Feminist to convey the pedagogical ideas and practices that this book promotes. Our interviewees gave their own interpretations of LGBT pedagogy, which reflect a multiplicity of perspectives. The nature of LGBT pedagogy is exemplified by the variety of responses offered below. Here are some samples of how the faculty we interviewed conceptualize LGBT pedagogy:

>> When I think of LGBT pedagogy, I think of intellectual and explicitly activist work that challenges heterosexism individually and institutionally, and most specifically, in the classroom (but beyond, of course). While folks in LGBT communities should be best able to speak to such contradictions, those of us who are straight have a bedrock responsibility to do this important work as well, especially if we want to "walk the walk" and not just "talk the talk" about making this a more humane and safe world.
>**>Winston Grady-Willis (African American Studies)**

>> LGBT pedagogy is the incorporation of LGBT issues into teaching. Topics of hate crimes, same-sex relationships, etc. should be discussed in the classroom. If a lecture is going to deal with issues of relationships, they should not just talk about relationships between men and women. These are not the only types of relationships that occur in the world.
>**>Jeremy Brunson (Sociology)**

>> [LGBT pedagogy] is a view of the world that always questions heterosexist norms and assumptions. It involves a process of asking questions about difference and how difference and diversity exist in our world and in our students' lives. It looks at the liminal spaces, those areas where people in various roles fall "betwixt and between" heteronormative assumptions. It is

107

a critical pedagogy, one that views sexuality from various approaches and critical lenses. It often intersects with other pedagogies of difference and diversity.
>**Paul Butler (The Writing Program)**

A lot of courses assume that LGBT pedagogy means just teaching about homophobia, but they don't teach about heteronormativity. And you cannot understand homophobia without understanding heteronormativity. A lot of my students feel that homophobia just means hate, fear, taboo, and they don't understand how they are complicit in keeping the norm of heteronormativity in place. Because they are not homophobic. They don't hate. They don't fear. So unless you also teach them about the norm of heterosexualism then they don't get what the problem is. They don't see the bigger picture.
>**Barbara Applebaum (Cultural Foundations of Education)**

I think of queer pedagogy as one that is disruptive of normative assumptions, troubles taken-for-granted assumptions, and is critical of binary thinking. Queer pedagogy confounds and confronts knowledge and power, exclusions, and erasures. It shifts the center and makes the familiar strange.
>**Beth Ferri (Teaching & Leadership/Cultural Foundations of Education)**

If you had to define [LGBT pedagogy], it would be any pedagogy that challenges heteronormativity. For me there's a pedagogy of student empowerment and involvement creating a "safe" space but also a space where students are willing to be challenged. But even those spaces can be heteronormative if a professor isn't aware of [her] own heteronormative perspectives, just like there can be racial and gender biases if you're not aware of how they're being produced.
>**Claudia Klaver (English)**

The way I imagine it is as a pedagogy that respects differences and permits people to name the world they live in. It uses people's naming of the world to say how the world is constructed.
>**Sari Knopp Biklen (Cultural Foundations of Education)**

LGBT pedagogy is giving students an opportunity to talk about the values and assumptions that they have and then presenting them with information and data that supports the kind of issues that are really happening with gays, lesbians, transgendered, and bisexual people.
>Kim Jaffee (Social Work)

It's a way of introducing material to students that allows them to see how the experience of this group of people relates to the subject matter that's being taught. And understanding how that experience may or may not be different than it is for the mainstream.
>Casey Sprock (College of Law)

To me, [this pedagogy] might entail a few qualities or characteristics, including (a) Constant querying/queerying—a curiosity that is active and that finds spaces to ask questions where there seems to be seamlessness: a deconstructive approach—this questioning must be self-directed as well as outer directed; (b) A thorough examination of the tools of power and dominance at work in the seeming innocence of dominant sexualities/condoned/legal practices/ identities; (c) A recognition that ALL sexuality NEVER takes place in a vacuum—it's always contextual, always imbricated with other identities, power matrices, vectors of culture, time place, space, nation: to me, queer pedagogy… must come to terms with how sexuality is intersectional and also historical rather than universal. This is important on two counts: one, to de-universalize/denaturalize the category of queerness or LGBT rather than perpetuate possible imperial/neocolonizing arrogance; (d) A recognition therefore that queer sexuality can be both a site of privilege and oppression BECAUSE it is interwoven with and located within other aspects of power and the self.
>Vivian May (Women's Studies)

As you can see from these varied comments, there is a wide range of ways to conceptualize LGBT/Queer pedagogy; however, there are some common elements upon which our informants concur. These include: acknowledging that we often make assumptions that the heterosexual experience is the "normal" experience; identifying and interrupting these assumptions; providing a supportive space for LGBT students; teaching about LGBT issues, but through a consideration of how these issues are related to heteronormativity, power, race, gender and other social categories; and finally, that this pedagogy is relevant to ALL TAs regardless of their own sexual orientation and regardless of their academic discipline. Before turning to the methods these teachers use in their practices of LGBT pedagogy, let's examine how heteronormativity relates to LGBT pedagogy.

Intersections of Heteronormativity and the "Work to be done"

As Aman Luthra points out in this volume, Syracuse University has made great strides in the interruption of heteronormative ideologies and practices on campus.[1] However, there is still work to be done. The notion of how heteronormativity is constructed and reinforced is not typically addressed in relation to diversity issues on campus or in the classroom. Changing this is an important element of our interviewees' thoughts about LGBT pedagogy. Jackie Orr (Sociology) says,

> The notion of social construction which says that things are not natural, that things are made through culture and history and relations of power, is extremely useful for trying to begin to destabilize … students' notion of sexual identity as natural and normal.

Orr's comment makes clear that recognizing the socially constructed nature of sexuality and gender (along with other social categories) is a powerful and necessary tool in the "work" to interrupt the power of dominant ideologies, including heteronormativity. Interrogating what is typically labeled "normal" and the resultant production of the "abnormal" centrally plays into this effort.

Another area of "work to be done" concerns the ways that LGBT issues ARE entering into the curriculum. While several departments administer courses addressing multiculturalism and diversity on campus and throughout society, the focus of these classes tends to emphasize race and ethnicity while comparatively little attention is given to issues that are specifically faced by the LGBT population. Plus, if attended to at all, LGBT issues are typically presented simply as one of many separate facets of "difference" among the population without acknowledgement of the cumulative effect people's sexual and gender identities often have on their entire social experience, or the ways that sexuality and gender intersect with other identity categories. If there is a disconnect between gender, sexuality, and the rest of a person's identities, this has the potential to minimize and invalidate a person's experience as a complete human being.

As Linda Carty (African American Studies) puts it:

> To simultaneously deal with the issues of gender, race, class, and sexuality is to recognize that some people experience multiple oppressions simultaneously. So, for example, if you have a woman who is a lesbian, black, and disabled, no one can deny that she would definitely experience more and multiple forms of oppression at the same time. So how can we talk about her without giving legitimacy to all of her? After all, she is never one part of herself without the others.

Carty reminds us that there are complex elements that interconnect in the construction of identity. How we, as instructors in the classroom, address these multifaceted components is likely to impact how our students self-identify as well as how they make sense of other peoples' self-concepts.

As a new TA, you may be wondering how you can begin working to recognize, minimize, and interrupt heteronormative practices in your teaching methods. The first step is to explore your own beliefs about lesbians, gay men, bisexuals, and transgendered people. What do you assume about your LGBT students and others with whom you interact? What do you feel when you think about LGBT people and LGBT issues? Why do you think that is? As Barbara Applebaum (Cultural Foundations of Education) states, "A professor who has not dealt with his or her own heteronormative assumptions...will be prevented from incorporating LGBT pedagogy... It's not a subject you can just teach and not understand yourself."

Holding biases and stereotypes about people whom you perceive as "different" from you are learned behaviors that are rooted in our socio-cultural context. Growth from and interruption of these biases is not a simple process; it involves a lot of critical reflection and intentional questioning. However, if you want to effectively teach diverse populations without subjecting them to your own personal biases, this reflection is required.

Disrupting heteronormativity in the curriculum and acknowledging the existence and effects of multiple oppressions can be a daunting task for TAs, but we have the responsibility to do so on a daily basis. You have made quite a bit of progress already by picking up this volume and increasing your awareness of LGBT pedagogical issues on campus. In the following sections, our faculty interviewees discuss ways that you can bridge this awareness with concrete teaching practices.

Recognizing Privilege and Disrupting Complacency: "Knocking you off your balance"

Many people are unaware of the many privileges they enjoy as a result of being born into a certain gender, class, race, or ethnic group. The same goes for those people who are straight *and* those who identify themselves as LGBT. As Vivian May (Women's Studies) observes, "Issues of class privilege and other privileges definitely play out in the classroom dynamic between teacher and student and among students. I think these unnamed power differentials and dynamics also can impact 'success' as a teacher."

Awareness of one's own social location and access to privilege is essential because you will be engaging with students who differ from you in terms of social categories that are directly related to power in this society, e.g., socioeconomic, racial, ethnic, religious, ability, sexual, age, and so on. Marj DeVault (Sociology) offers this example of "catching herself" using concepts or language that reinforced power and privilege, as opposed to disrupting them:

> Very, very early in my teaching, when I was teaching a course called Sociology of Women, a woman stopped me and corrected me, "It sounds like you are really only talking about heterosexuals." And that surprised me... it also really got me thinking—so one of the things that I have done ever since is to continually try to catch myself.

You must be conscious of where you stand in the greater scheme of things, how your worldview and life experiences may differ radically from those of your students, and how your assumptions about particular cultural practices or populations are formed from your own social location.

At the same time, teachers need to develop a sense of the ways in which students express their social privilege in the classroom (knowingly or not) and be able to call attention to these instances in a manner that generates productive and challenging discussions. "When [students] communicate their privilege without knowing it," Sari Knopp Biklen (Cultural Foundations of Education) observes, "you have to address it. In my research methods class, I talk about needing to know your social location before doing research so you know how you're interpreting the readings and the data."

Beth Ferri (Teaching and Leadership and Cultural Foundations of Education) addresses privilege as a hindrance to the transformative power of education:

> I don't know if I am ever completely successful with trying to denaturalize privilege, especially when students—especially students occupying the normative center—expect the classroom to be a "safe place." I don't necessarily have that expectation. I think education, when it is transformative, always knocks you off balance, which feels anything but safe. Of course, students who do not occupy such places of privilege often do not have the privilege of assuming that the classroom will be a safe place. When teachers and students talk about the classroom as a safe space, I wonder—safe for whom?

Despite these concerns about creating safe space in the classroom, it is an important component of LGBT pedagogy. Linda Alcoff (Philosophy) emphasizes the importance of "making the classroom safe enough for students to express differences in opinion and yet make sure that you are not letting certain kinds of ignorant statements of hatred pass by...it's like treading a thin line."

Barbara Applebaum (Cultural Foundations of Education) helps her students recognize the privilege held by those in the mainstream through a classroom exercise in which she asks her students to recap their weekend activities with their loved ones for 10-15 minutes. After a short debriefing, she reminds them that not everyone can speak so freely about their loved ones. Many heterosexual students do not realize what a privilege it is for them to be able to openly express their affection for their loved ones, such as walking hand-in-hand down the street or sharing a simple kiss.

Claudia Klaver (English) throws her students off balance by first making it known that she has a daughter before coming out as a lesbian at some point in the semester. Jackie Orr (Sociology) uses the interesting technique of referring to both heterosexuals and LGBT people as "us," a method that makes her own sexuality ambiguous. "I talk to TAs who want to know what it means," she observes, " ...they don't necessarily hear when I say 'we' when I talk about heterosexuals."

Methods like these are employed by many faculty members to directly challenge students' ignorance and stereotyping that "usually stem from the belief that they do not know anyone who is queer. It is important to recognize this type of naivety. It is this type of naivety that makes it more important to address these issues" (Jeremy Brunson, Sociology). Lauren Eastwood (Sociology) cites an example of this naivety during a classroom discussion in which a student assumed that gay people are not contributing to population growth because they don't have babies. Eastwood interrupted the misconception and assumptions of heteronormativity by pointing out that gay people might not biologically have babies with their partners, but they can and do have and raise children.

You have to make the (classroom) safe enough for students to express differences in opinion and yet make sure that you are not letting certain kinds of ignorant statements of hatred pass by. In that way students start to see a particular teacher as someone with a vested interest in a matter such as sexuality.

>Linda Alcoff (Philosophy)

How is LGBT Pedagogy Relevant to My Discipline?

It may seem that LGBT issues can be discarded by some disciplines as irrelevant to their content. However, as Ahoura Afshar argues in this volume, the relevance of LGBT issues exists in every classroom, for every discipline, and for every instructor at Syracuse University.[2] This is due, in part, to the ways that heteronormativity operates, but also due to the responsibility we all have as instructional staff at Syracuse University.

Our faculty respondents do agree that LGBT issues are most easily engaged in the social sciences and humanities, and that these issues are more difficult to envision as "relevant" to other disciplines, especially the "hard" sciences or "technical" disciplines. Linda Carty (African American Studies) reminds us, "The literature has shown that in higher education, particularly in the natural sciences, issues of race, gender, sexuality and difference are not adequately addressed." This finding reflects a problem with the way that the content of these disciplines remains unchallenged, not that issues and ideologies pertaining to social differences are irrelevant. In treating LGBT issues as simply a matter of subject content in the curriculum, we fail to adequately take into consideration the deeper issue of heteronormativity, which is ever present in all disciplines and in every classroom.

As Beth Ferri (Teaching and Leadership and Cultural Foundations of Education) asserts, "I can't think of a discipline that does not deal with difference, binaries, or normative assumptions. Classrooms are inherently political spaces—who speaks, who listens, whose worldview is taken as universal and natural? Whose knowledge counts and who counts as a knower? These are all reflective of power." In this sense, LGBT issues are relevant to all disciplines, because of the inherent heteronomativity that prevails in most socio-cultural contexts.

Paul Butler (Writing Program) points out that the sciences are prone to viewing "societal institutions and practices through a heteronormative lens" without considering examples that include LGBT persons. Butler goes on to argue, "Most instructors feel they don't have the knowledge or ability [to do so]. They may feel it's important, but they don't have the resources or examples of creative ways in which it has been brought into other courses." Linda Alcoff (Philosophy) adds, "What is interesting is that students are often inclined and committed to issues of equality and fairness but they have not had an opportunity to do any systematic thinking about heterosexism and homophobia."

In addition, Vivian May (Women's Studies) asserts:

> Classrooms are not free of dominant social paradigms or power dynamics—they are sites of nation building and normalizing. And, although many of us struggle against these imperatives in our work, we are still working within sets of assumptions about education as a neutral, liberal democratic endeavor but not necessarily as the practice of freedom and overtly politicized space of unthinking/rethinking hegemony.

May argues that all disciplines do touch upon sexuality issues at some point, listing such disparate fields as economics, history, law, policy studies, art, athletics, and religion. Lauren Eastwood (Sociology) offers an interesting example of institutionalized heteronormativity in the natural sciences contained within a physics textbook. Within the text, an illustration depicts "attraction of molecules" in terms of a plus/minus binary. The illustration shows a picture of a woman under the plus sign and a picture of a man under the minus symbol. The next frame depicts "contraction" and shows two men as the minus/minus relationship of contraction, the opposite of attraction. Here, the assumption of heterosexuality illustrates this physics concept, while also reinforcing heteronormative understandings of the world.

As Eastwood's example demonstrates, heteronormativity can innocently appear in any textbook, and TAs need to be able to recognize this and to interrupt it as often as possible. When TAs can recognize heteronormativity, interrogate it, and teach against it, our students, in turn, can learn to recognize and interrupt it. As TAs, we have the ability to incorporate the ideas and examples from this volume into our pedagogical methods. In the following section of this essay, our interviewees discuss examples of their own pedagogical practices.

Best Practices in LGBT pedagogy

As alluded to in some of the examples above, one of the most effective ways to begin interrupting heteronormative assumptions in the classroom is to critically analyze the examples used in class discussion for their relation to heteronormative ideologies.

Using examples to interrupt heteronormativity

Heteronormativity on campus is often reinforced through such innocuous practices as using male-female examples and analogies in instructional examples. For TAs, tailoring our classroom examples to include LGBT concepts is one of the easiest and most effective ways we can disrupt heteronormativity and show that we recognize and support LGBT relationships. Casey Sprock (College of Law) designs his classroom examples to include same-sex partners in business and law (not necessarily in romantic relationships) to illustrate people of the same sex "working toward the same goal and building something together." He also uses examples of same-sex couples rather than the heterosexual married couples most often used to illustrate course concepts.

In a similar way, Kim Jaffee (Social Work) relates an example from her classes on social work and domestic violence:

> Many times domestic violence, as opposed to intimate partner violence, makes an assumption that it is a married couple, a man and a wife, in a marital relationship or heterosexual marital relationship and so I move to using the

terminology of "intimate partner violence." This method allows me to talk about studies which use the hetero terminology but in fact I reinterpret that in order to create a climate that is open to relationships of all kinds.

Jaffee uses opportunities like these to critically interpret the assumptions in the literature and debunk the myths that relationships are always heterosexual.

In mathematics, word problems provide many opportunities for reinterpreting the classroom example to interrupt heteronormativity. For example, a reframing of a standard word problem might read: "Bill and Tom bought a car for $23,000 and financed it for 7.5% over 3 years. Figure out the monthly payments they will have to make." Even though you're not explicitly discussing same-sex relationships, you are letting students know that you're comfortable with the fact that people other than heterosexuals do things together and have relationships. This is an important concept to convey to students who may not be accustomed to that idea.

I have been forever changed as a teacher whose first job was in the Bible Belt. I had to develop a kind of "coyote" pedagogy to bring things in from the side door (to avoid student resistance). I don't think this is less political, but it is different and in other contexts may not be recognized as a queering/political strategy...

>Vivian May (Women's Studies)

Jeremy Brunson (Sociology) provides the following example for a marketing class. In discussions about supply and demand, you can easily talk about the marketability of gay and lesbian characters on prime time television. Here, a focus on LGBT people as a marketing niche works effectively as part of the larger discussion of marketing issues. Without having to state a political position, or "deal with LGBT issues," you affirm the reality of gay people in the marketplace and also affirm the presence of and support for LGBT people in your classroom.

For an African American Studies class, Linda Carty suggests that discussions about important figures such as feminist activist Audre Lorde, poet and novelist James Baldwin, or civil rights activist Bayard Rustin, should include some discussion of their sexual orientation as integral to their personal and political struggle. In this way, you reinforce the point that one's intersectional identities are important to understanding political and social movements as well as one's creative practice.

Challenging Assumptions

A second pedagogical practice involves challenging the assumptions that you hear from your students. The contributors to this volume are committed to the belief that an important component of responsible pedagogy is attention to students' critical thinking skills. This involves challenging unfounded and inflammatory statements and assumptions as they arise in the classroom. As Jackie Orr (Sociology) points out, "increasingly, the students who are embodying or saying things that I think are sexist, heterosexist, racist, or homophobic [are] doing it with a kind of hegemonic confidence that I find incredibly disturbing and does make me think, as an educator…what I want to do in my classroom is promote unlearning." Leading a critical and thoughtful classroom discussion in order to help your students (and you) unlearn these unfounded biases and oppressive assumptions, without having it devolve into a mindless recitation of dogmatic rhetoric, is a crucial teaching skill that develops with practice. Karen Hall (English) offers this example:

> Think of a moment when you knew something and your mother didn't and it was embarrassing for you. Whether you were at a football game and your mother didn't understand what a linebacker did, or whether you were in a math tournament and she didn't understand what calculus was. There is something, some illiteracy that your mother has, [that has] made you feel embarrassed. So that even if my students are strongly from the center of social power and norms, then I'll use that experience and help them then connect out from it…So I start from what they do know and I respect it and invite them to bring it into the room in a critical way so that they start to be reflective of their subject position.

Hall's assignment offers students a way to begin to look at their (unconscious) assumptions, but in a non-threatening way that invites them to become self reflective and self-critical.

118

It is important to remember not to be reactive, lest we denigrate our students and lose their attention completely. As Claudia Klaver (English) puts it, "I don't call the comments 'homophobic' or 'racist' because to do that is to call the student that. ... I try to 'complicate' it. Nobody really says anything explicitly racist or homophobic, but they do make assumptions." When students make comments that reflect their ignorance on these matters, Paul Butler (Writing Program) suggests:

> I ask students to examine what's at the root of some of their responses and beliefs. I also allow the students in the class to monitor some of the responses. I find that students usually handle these kinds of comments with a great deal of sophistication and complexity. I think it's important to address these comments and probe deeply, yet I must say that in general the number of these comments is minimal. I think it's important to establish a classroom environment in which conflict can be addressed openly.

Butler's suggestions are echoed in a wide range of responses from faculty about their own efforts to provide constructive and transformative learning environments.

What are some of these teachers' approaches to the challenge of managing an effective classroom discussion while also promoting critical examination of inflammatory and offensive remarks?

>> I encourage students to bring out these differences because they are there. Don't say it outside of class and not say it in class. I know that they come to classes like mine with certain inherited assumptions and I want them to be aware of those. I encourage them to challenge the authors, challenge the professor, and challenge each other. All they have to do is substantiate their challenge with legitimate sources. They must show that they have read and understood the course materials and that they found other sources that refuted these. With this openness and encouragement I don't have problems of resistance merely for the sake of resistance. Students learn that oftentimes their common sense knowledge of the world is inaccurate and needs revising. I would welcome the most reactionary students...because I know that I will transform their thinking.

>Linda Carty (African American Studies)

>> I try to nip all kinds of phobic comments in the bud: challenge them and point out their inappropriate nature for my classroom or any class, for that matter. Offer counterarguments, turn questions around, use humor.
>**Vivian May (Women's Studies)**

>> When students make comments that deny their privilege, it is the responsibility of instructors to expose such contradictions in a constructive way. This often means engaging in class discussions that allow other students to "check" such comments before those of us at the rostrum open our mouths. Another thing that helps is honesty. I tell students time and time again that my own homophobia as a young Black man was the key reason why I became estranged from one of the best friends I ever had growing up.
>**Winston Grady-Willis (African American Studies)**

>> The instructor has to model appropriate classroom discourse. I make sure that I do not make arguments that are abusive or targeted at any student. And I encourage my students to do the same thing. Second, the instructor has to maintain some control over the discussion. This is often tricky for new teachers (or TAs). You have to strike a balance in which students feel free to express their views, but within the bounds of appropriateness. You don't want a class that is silent, and you don't want a class that is totally out of control. And you need to anticipate when the class is veering toward a hostile direction so that you can prevent that from happening. The point is to elicit responses, and yet maintain decorum. In other words, I am in favor of maintaining a structured environment of dialogue and discussion.
>**Thomas Keck (Political Science)**

>> In my class there is Zero Indifference. If someone comes up with a homophobic, racist, or sexist remark, we stop everything and whether there is silence, we challenge it and try to deconstruct it. ...I'll tell them to come see me after class unless I think it's helpful for the whole class. But one problem I have in my classroom, and it's always a challenge, is very religious people that say [homosexuality is] a sin. Because I am an Orthodox Jew, they are actually in shock when I don't accept that as an answer. One of the things I

have done in class is I say, "You go home tonight and you tell me honestly, think in the heart of your hearts how much you actually believe it's a sin, that being gay is a sin, and how much you actually fear and can't deal with it because it threatens your sexuality and then come back to me next week and we'll talk about it again." Because a lot of them hide behind the religious rationalization. A lot of fear that they don't want to face and when they face that we can talk.
>**Barbara Applebaum (Cultural Foundations of Education)**

There is often a muted reaction whenever there is a discussion of heterosexism and homophobia in class. ...this silence indicates discomfort. I try a technique in which the students don't have to come out and take a stand one way or another. I ask them: "What are the major arguments against homosexuality?" And slowly, they would start to talk about these things without claiming that they have these views themselves. Sometimes, just to get them started, I also lay out the major arguments and then ask them if I have missed out on something. That way they can point out what they think or have heard without taking on the personal culpability of being homophobic.
>**Linda Alcoff (Philosophy)**

I have, occasionally, had students express problematic comments in class and in online class discussions. I typically confront such comments and say why I think they could be offensive. Sometimes students do not realize that they have said something that could be hurtful and appreciate having the opportunity to discuss it. Others feel ashamed although this is not my intent. And still others think that I am just being "PC" and deny that what they said is problematic. My goal is simply to have students question their taken-for-granted assumptions and to be critical of thinking that their reality is shared or universal.
>**Beth Ferri (Teaching & Leadership/Cultural Foundations of Education)**

To address when students are seemingly caught in their own stereotyping, one of the things that I've done is to have students analyze something outside of class—they see a film or go to a presentation in light of the class material.

121

I call it a "stretch exercise" where they are supposed to look at how this might be applicable to the outside world. Lo and behold! They find themselves doing something that critiques heteronormativity through that process.
>**Lauren Eastwood (Sociology)**

The main thing I do when people say really racist, sexist, or homophobic things is not have a really big reaction. …this is weird because it's like creating a safe space for homophobia, but I'm not really talking about a safe space. I'm trying to create a space where interesting conversation can happen, not really stupid, boring, prefabricated conversation. And so, I remain calm and respond with a question, and I always respond from the position of a sociologist.
>**Jackie Orr (Sociology)**

What I would normally do to intervene is to ask questions. You know, open-ended questions to get the student to start to talk and then rely on the rest of the class and the readings to support whatever position I felt the need to take. And if the student becomes belligerent, to say, "Well, I feel like you're crossing the line and we're not having an intellectual discussion and we need to stop." And then, of course, the thing is to not…let them push your buttons. Because at that point…it's a power game.
>**Karen Hall (English)**

It is important to keep in mind that not all student resistance is due to bigotry or homophobia. There are many psychological, sociological, and environmental factors affecting the development of all your students, LGBT and straight. Sometimes the ignorance or opposition might be resistance for its own sake, or maybe, for the student, it is an exercise in debate, intellectual discussion, and questioning authority. As Karen Hall (English) observes:

Who knows what's triggered this person? Maybe it's homophobia…the most important thing for me in dealing with the "problem student" is to really remind myself that I do not know what the problem is. If I assume it's sexuality or my sexuality, I am making myself far more important than I probably am.

Don't be quick to judge the student as a bigot, but always be ready to engage all students in challenging and critical intellectual examinations of inaccurate assumptions and beliefs. Never let inflammatory comments "slip by."

Being a Visible LGBT Ally

Being an ally to both LGBT and straight students can interrupt heteronormativity in powerful and complex ways. The first step is understanding what an ally actually is.[3] Lauren Eastwood (Sociology) defines an LGBT "ally" as "someone who could be gay or could not but either way you're supportive of these issues." One of the easiest ways to demonstrate your status as an LGBT ally is by displaying the "Safe Space" sticker, which you see prominently placed on many faculty members' doors. However, this is merely a symbolic gesture that must be backed up with action, when you are ready to do so.

I think one thing that keeps instructors from handling things is fear – because they imagine these issues in stark binaries or stark contrasts in perspectives. The more you know about these issues, the more ways you have in addressing the issues and how they connect with your subject matter, the less fearful people are.

>Sari Knopp Biklen (Cultural Foundations of Education)

Several faculty argue that you need to let people know you are an ally "by word and example" (Casey Sprock) and through the language you use (Jeremy Brunson). Others more explicitly include LGBT issues in their curriculum. Sari Knopp Biklen (Cultural Foundations of Education) routinely assigns texts by gay and lesbian authors, includes sexuality as a significant identity marker in her teachings, supports the work of her LGBT students, and regularly raises heteronormativity in her classes as an issue for consideration.

Vivian May (Women's Studies) advocates participating in conversations about relevant LGBT issues with your students, communicating with your students via e-mail, bringing up LGBT topics and questions in class, offering extra credit for examining LGBT issues, and sometimes discussing one's own life experiences. Paul

Butler (Writing Program) displays his alliance by refusing to hide his own sexual orientation from his students. He not only makes it known that he is gay, but he also brings up issues in the classroom that relate to the LGBT community. He reports that his students tend to respond to his openness by sharing relevant examples from their own lives.

Sometimes dramatic scenes play out before your eyes and it is up to you, the instructor, to handle the situation with compassion and wisdom. Winston Grady-Willis (African American Studies) relates a powerful classroom experience that indisputably named his identity as an LGBT ally:

> Two years ago a White student (who I later found out was gay) asked a straight-to-the- point question during a discussion about the lynching of Blacks in the apartheid South. "Do you consider the murder of Matthew Shepherd to be a lynching?" Everyone's eyes focused on him, and then on me, when I responded. "Absolutely," I said. "Matthew Shepherd was the victim of a lynching, just like James Byrd." The answer was a simple one for me. Both men were the victims of group murder and torture by individuals who considered themselves inherently superior, and yet, who felt threatened by their respective victims in the most intimate ways. ...Everyone knew where I stood.

Barbara Applebaum (Cultural Foundations of Education) adds this wisdom about students who come out to her privately.

> I speak out in class so at least they know I'm an advocate. People have come out to me in journals, but I know they don't want to come out to the classroom, and that's perfectly fine. I understand that. I can't make the classroom a safe place for them no matter how much I try...I hope that it makes them at least feel safe with me.

Being an ally demands that you take some risks, yes, but more importantly that you attempt to make your classroom as safe as possible for all students.

A related issue regarding being an ally concerns recognizing and respecting the intersections of identity categories in your students and yourself. Linda Carty (African

American Studies) noted earlier that you cannot begin to understand the experiences of a person until you consider all aspects of that person's identity. This identity includes the person's sexuality, age, gender, ability, race, ethnicity, and socioeconomic status, among other categories. These traits and social locations combine to create a unique individual who is more than the sum of her parts, or merely a patchwork of non-intersecting components. We all have intersecting identities and related experiences that are useful when we're relating to other people. Here are some ways in which SU faculty acknowledge these intersections and use them to enhance their teaching methods:

>> As a below-the-knee amputee who wears a prosthesis, I have had to come to terms with the fact that I, especially when younger, passed as able-bodied. The issue of passing is central to the lives of many in the LGBT community, too, of course, as well as for those in other contexts (e.g. some very light-complexioned Blacks in the US, some Jews in Europe and here in the US). So perhaps, too, from my own personal experiences as a Black male who is also heterosexual and disabled, alliances have been drawn.
>Winston Grady-Willis (African American Studies)

>> We have intersecting identities. I had a guy who wrote to me in his journal, "you know as a gay person I never realized that I could be oppressive to somebody else because I am white." And it was the perfect moment to show... I am oppressed because I am a woman but that doesn't mean I can't be dominant because I'm white... These intersections are what sometimes prevent us from seeing some of the ways in which we contribute to oppression.
>Barbara Applebaum (Cultural Foundations of Education)

>> All these categories must be understood to intersect with other issues of difference, social inequality, and power. This means however that sometimes students don't recognize anything "queer" going on, or they feel that everything is "queer" or "raced" but not enough about "women." ... Student locations factor in a lot as does the professor's.
>Vivian May (Women's Studies)

Finding similarities and making connections with other people aids the instructor in making genuine connections with students and creating inclusive and relevant examples in the classroom. This is an integral part of making it known to your students that you are a LGBT ally. Aside from being an ally, you may be wondering if it is necessary to be gay to best cultivate LGBT pedagogy, or if you need to have a specific theoretical background, such as feminist theory, to do this work. We asked our faculty informants for their perspective on these issues.

Do you need to be LGBT to practice this pedagogy?

Linda Carty (African American Studies) argues that one does not have to be gay.

> That's like saying that only black people can talk about racism because they are so often victimized by it. But we must remember that the perpetrators of racism are responsible for its maintenance... We all have a responsibility to address these issues where and when necessary.

Barbara Applebaum (Cultural Foundations of Education) concurs:

> I definitely don't think you have to [be LGBT] and I think sometimes when you have predominantly heterosexual students it's better not to be. It's better to be "het." Then they don't use that line, "Well, you have an agenda so I can dismiss what you're saying."

Applebaum underscores a major theme of this volume: we all have a responsibility to engage LGBT pedagogy, regardless of our sexual orientation. Vivian May (Women's Studies) adds:

> I really hate the idea of limiting who can "do" LGBT pedagogy based on identity, discipline, etc. I feel that plays into the dominant logics that have helped to maintain marginalization for all kinds of people.

May argues that limiting LGBT pedagogy to those who are LGBT is problematic for the very work to be done. Jeremy Brunson (Sociology), however, points out that his particular position sometimes becomes central to the examples he uses:

As a gay man who is in a position of authority, I have often found it difficult to merge my responsibility to educate with making students feel comfortable in the classroom. A lot of my examples in class are from personal experience or are very close to me. I often have to remind myself that coming out might not be the best way to get my point across. Although I do have it in the back of my mind, I will say that I have never remained closeted out of this concern. There are times, that I have "outed" myself while making a point and felt completely comfortable with my decision.

For Brunson, being gay makes it easier to do this work. For Barbara Applebaum, however, identifying as heterosexual enables her to incorporate LGBT pedagogy more effectively in her classrooms. Clearly, these faculty feel that anyone who is committed to responsible teaching, regardless of sexual orientation, can be effective practitioners of LGBT pedagogy.

Do you need to be a feminist to do this work?

Many of our faculty believe that being a feminist helps in the practice of LGBT pedagogy, but it is certainly not a requirement. Barbara Applebaum (Cultural Foundations of Education) suggests: "You don't have to be a feminist, but you have to understand oppression in a more macro perspective." Other faculty comment:

> I am a feminist, and that certainly informs my teaching of LGBT issues. But, do you have to be a feminist to do so? I'm not sure. I'm happy to entertain the possibility that a teacher might not be a feminist and also teach LGBT content successfully. There are certainly some LGBT rights advocates who are anti-feminist, pro-life, etc.
> **>Thomas Keck (Political Science)**

> I certainly think that it helps when someone embraces feminist politics unapologetically. In the given moment here at SU, in Syracuse, and in the larger world in terms of all sorts of politics, the reality oftentimes is that someone who sees "feminism" as a dirty word probably isn't going to embrace the notion of LGBT pedagogy. Those, like womanist scholars, who see the term feminism as being problematic at a definitional level but who also

challenge gendered structured in their work, can and do teach LGBT pedagogy. >**Winston Grady-Willis (African American Studies)**

>> Do you have to be a feminist pedagogical practitioner? To some degree, yes, you do, because I think if you are feminist it means that you critically analyze gender and power.
>**Karen Hall (English)**

Why might a feminist orientation be considered important, by some faculty members, to practicing effective LGBT pedagogy? Feminist theorists critically examine the power relations embedded in social constructs of gender, race, sexuality, ability, class, and so on. These social constructs create and reinforce, feminists argue, hierarchies of power and profound inequities in our cultural structures and institutions. Processes that naturalize and normalize systems of privilege are integral to masking and thus maintaining dominant ideologies and practices. The themes that feminist theorists address include deconstructing the traditional societal power structures, addressing issues of implicit and explicit oppression by the dominant culture, and interrogating the intersections of oppression around social categories. As the previous statements indicate, many of our faculty interviewees believe that critical thinking skills are essential for developing students' abilities to uncover their "naturalized" beliefs and assumptions and to critically reflect on the effects of these beliefs on individual and structural practices.

Although the faculty interviewed for this volume indicate that identifying as LGBT and/or feminist may help one's efforts to engage in LGBT pedagogy, it is essential that every teacher committed to responsible pedagogical practices—heterosexual or LGBT, non-feminist or feminist—understand that she or he can and must do this work.

Conclusion

>> At the institutional level, the University has at least three responsibilities: (a) guaranteeing a safe environment for LGBT students; (b) supporting LGBT student organizations; and (c) encouraging the incorporation of LGBT issues into the curriculum. I think the creation of a LGBT Studies (or Queer Studies) minor or major would be a great step. I am looking forward to further progress in this regard.
>**Thomas Keck (Political Science)**

As members of the future professoriate, we have a strong responsibility to address issues of inequality whenever possible. Indeed, this is a part of the core mission of Syracuse University. Responsible teachers recognize diversity in all its forms and construct our pedagogical methods to challenge invisible systems of privilege that perpetuate the exclusion of "non-mainstream" students from our curriculum and classroom practices. Learning to recognize and interrupt systems of privilege and normalcy in our own beliefs and teaching practices, as well as in students' beliefs and practices, is essential to creating responsible and reflexive teaching and learning environments.

The use of the conscientious pedagogical techniques and "best practices" described by the faculty interviewed for this book should serve as a guide to new TAs from those who have "been there" and are familiar with the terrain of the SU landscape. Whether you identify yourself as LGBT or not, your actions in and out of the classroom as a TA and an LGBT ally will have lasting effects on the lives of the students you teach. Take an active role in the changing face of higher education in America. Your students, the campus environment, and society at large will all benefit. There's no telling where your influence will end. See you in the classroom.

>>The author would like to thank Nisha Gupta for her substantial help with re-organization and revision of this essay.

>>Endnotes

1 > See "(Un)Straightening the Syracuse University Landscape" in this volume.
2 > See "The Invisible Presence of Sexuality in the Classroom" in this volume.
3 > See "The Importance of LGBT Allies" in this volume.

Toward a LGBT Studies Minor

Margaret Himley, Adrea Jaehnig, and
Andrew London, with comments from
Jonathan Massey

On March 9, 2004 Adrea Jaehnig initiated a conversation among members of the Senate Committee on LGBT Concerns, which focused on their ideas about LGBT pedagogy and designing and implementing a minor in LGBT Studies at Syracuse University. Over the past two years, the committee has been talking with others on campus, sponsoring nationally recognized LGBT speakers, hosting a faculty reading group, and planning for a fall 2004 conference on LGBT Studies with the goal of enlarging the number of course offerings that focus on or include LGBT scholarship. The committee has also been considering the promises and potential pitfalls of an organized minor in LGBT Studies. The conversation that follows reflects some of the thoughts and concerns of committee members.

AJ: Let's start our conversation about LGBT pedagogy and see where it goes from there.

MH: I have two different contexts for thinking about this. I used to teach LGBT Studies and the Rhetoric of AIDS as elective courses in the English Department, and I have raised LGBT issues and theories in our required writing courses. And I think in both contexts there are three landmines. One is that teachers worry that they don't know enough to do justice to the large and interdisciplinary field of LGBT Studies. To explain one thing, you have to explain many, many, many things, and you may end up giving such a reductive version of it all that it is not actually helpful.

>>key>>>>>>>>>

MH: Margaret Himley
AJ: Adrea Jaehnig
AL: Andrew London

AL: Yes, when I taught Sociology of Gays and Lesbians, I really struggled with how to organize the curriculum because the field had changed a lot. So you want to give some history, right? And allow them to read sort of in depth. But then if you are doing that, it is hard to do it across lots of topics. So I really struggled with how to represent the field as it is changing even within a single discipline. And then you start to do that across disciplines...and it is really hard to capture the field, even though I agree that it is a well-established interdisciplinary field.

MH: And it is also a social movement, and much of what goes on is happening at the level of social movement. A lot of the transgender work is happening not because there is academic research going on, although there is some of that, but because there are people who are living their lives on the front lines and making very big demands on legal and health care systems.

AL: There is also the media and cultural aspect, so a lot of what the students are bringing into class with them is this popular mis-knowledge or superficial knowledge, and you're trying to tie that to scholarship that has a history and a disciplinary location. Doing all of that is just really, really hard.

MH: Especially if you have to do it all in one course. The students come from different disciplines and have no shared vocabulary or knowledge base. And they also come with identity politics needs. In my courses, about half the students were LGBT, and it was exciting for them to have a class focused on queer life and work. And you don't want to displace that desire in some way or turn it cynical with critical theory, so you've got all of these competing needs going on.

AL: And then half your class is probably straight, so they don't have even so much of the taken for granted stuff from popular culture. A lot of my students had never even heard of Stonewall before. Just even this basic 101 stuff isn't available to a lot of the students but then you have a few students who know everything.

AJ: That's right. This makes me think about the project that we have done with the Newhouse School, where we had to give some background and information. Even that was very limited. Think just about trans issues, which has turned gender on its head. In order to really answer questions about trans people or the trans movement, you really need a whole class!

AL: Yes, this idea of just infusing it as a topical issue without any context or history, without any connection to ideas of gender and sexuality...I mean, it doesn't do it justice.

MH: Without an analytical approach to sexuality and gender, it is really hard to answer a question about what a trans person is. The answer requires a lot of theory and history and discourse.

AJ: Before the Trans Teach-In, people would ask me how many transgender people there are on campus. You know, you could think maybe a handful, but now my answer is, it depends on how you define transgender. What's the second landmine?

MH: The second one is much easier – that's the whole fear of political correctness suppressing real dialogue and inquiry. And the third problem is moralism, where taking up LGBT issues means, let's learn to be nice to them, which is just a sentimental form of othering. It doesn't move the center at all. It assumes that we should just make that liberal gesture of inclusion because those 'other people' are having such a hard time. When someone says something that is transphobic or homophobic in class and the teacher says something like, 'Well that's not very nice,' that seems like the wrong response to me. It lends itself to setting up the demand to be tolerant. It positions the dominant student as thinking, 'I need to be generous and this is just something that I can do, because I am mainstream.'

AJ: Because you still have the power. Power doesn't shift at all.

MH: Right, and you're not touched by them or the questions they raise.

AJ: Which is like the Tunnel of Oppression.[1]

We need more people who are talking about (LGBT issues) and it needs to be faculty.

>SU undergraduate student

MH: Which is like the Tunnel of Oppression problem. Here is this person's problem, and that person's problem, and oh …I feel so badly for them, because I am such a nice person, and I

134

wish their life were easier. As if all gay people and trans people were just miserable all the time. They become objects of pity.

AJ: And who wants to be pitied?

MH: And then you have a politics that is not about desire and pleasure – the joys of collective work and imagination and utopic dreams, as in Robin D. G. Kelley's *Freedom Dreams: The Black Radical Imagination.*

AL: So is this conversation becoming an argument for having more classes that are taught by faculty who have that same sort of vision, orientation, and capacity as opposed to doing a broad infusion?

MH: Ah, this takes up back to the question of whether we want a minor in LGBT Studies. I don't know finally where I am going to land on that question. I suspect that I am going to land in favor of it. For example, I have loved how the LGBT Studies Faculty Reading Seminar has been set up around debates and tensions and pleasant disciplinary disagreement. I would love to see an introductory, cross disciplinary LGBT Studies course organized around history, identity, and social movements, and the unsettling of gender and sexuality. Debate draws people in.

AL: I feel like this is a moment historically and institutionally to define for ourselves a LGBT minor. I also want to build relationships with other programs on campus like Women's Studies, but I don't want to be subsumed with anything else as a structure.

AJ: I like the idea too of the minor including projects and activist work. I think there is way too much separation between what happens in the classroom and what is happening locally. Students don't experience that separation. They are actively thinking about what's happening in Pride Union or the student center or hearing about another black face incident or gay bashing and wondering how that all connects to the curriculum and what is happening or not happening in the classroom. A lot of students want to talk about these issues in classes and not in politically correct ways. This generation of students is bringing a whole other level of understanding of sexuality and gender. I think that they could be teaching us things and probably will, if we are open to that and are creating space for that to happen. All of this stuff is shifting in radical ways, and it's hard to believe we're not studying this and there isn't space in the curriculum to do that.

AL: I think that creating space is my major argument for having a minor. It creates a specific location. I am still for infusing, but infusing means giving up a lot of control. I think balancing infusion with a location where students are getting more theoretical grounding allows them to challenge and change those other environments that aren't working for them. There has to be a place too for LGBT scholars.

MH: I am very optimistic that these courses would be exciting for people, that there would be energy generated around them, that there would be pressure on enrollment, and that other people would want to be come a part of it. The minor could be a center of cutting edge work in a lot of disciplines.

AL: My experience of doing interdisciplinary teaching, however, has been that interdisciplinary classes look great on paper but they are harder to do in practice. I can imagine some people having a really hard time teaching in an interdisciplinary context.

MH: There is the fear of creating a structure that becomes untenable because it's geared for particular people. Institutionalizing the minor also might mean that one year you are arguing for the changes in the sex and gender system and the next you are arguing about how you are going to get a Xerox machine.

AJ: It loses its transformational power.

AL: When you look at institutionalization, there is always that trade off.

MH: But the Senate Committee cannot keep doing this. It will not maintain the high level of work. It is having trouble maintaining even now. We want some faculty lines, and we need some resources dedicated to this kind of work if the university is serious about it.

AJ: And we want it seen not as this minoritizing approach to a particular group of people, but as issues that cut across every aspect of our lives – all of our lives, not just the LGBT students.

MH: So do we want to call the minor Sexuality Studies?

AL: As opposed to naming it LGBT? We would likely gain a bigger audience, and politically it would be more palatable.

MH: Do we lose the LGBT students then?

AL: We might. But if we name it Sexuality Studies and then have specific LGBT courses, I think that would be fine.

AJ: You may lose some people, and you may gain others. There are so many ways that calling the center the LGBT Resource Center limits who feels like this is a place where they can come. But at the same time, it has also created space that didn't exist before, and not just here but in so many different places on campuses. There has been a proliferation of new groups – the gay fraternity, the faculty LGBT reading group, the LGBT people of color group called Fusion. Those are three things that pretty much happened this semester.

There is also great value in disruption. The context in which we are operating is so heavily regulated by heteronormativity that calling this minor Sexuality Studies could so easily make LGBT invisible. While I agree that one of our principles is inclusiveness, I also believe that one of our goals is disruption and transformation of normal. I would rather go with Queer Studies than Sexuality Studies, which is both inclusive and disruptive.

Comments (Jonathan Massey):

After reviewing this conversation, I would like to add some comments and observations. My sense is that "having our own place" – institutional as well as curricular – is crucial. I think some kind of program, even if without a minor, is very important. In addition to the issues of control, serving student needs, and getting a revenue stream, I would raise another: expertise. The problem with infusion, as is noted above, is the difficulty of ensuring the quality of the teaching across a wide spectrum of faculty members. It seems to me that a core of faculty who already have the needed expertise, or who are willing to develop it as part of participating in a program, is crucial for establishing scholarly rigor in this field. That could be complemented by an "infusion" initiative wherein we ask key members in many disciplines to develop a secondary expertise in LGBT issues within their field. We would ask them to integrate this new expertise into their teaching. These faculty members would then become models and "diffusers" of LGBT knowledge, and the integration of that knowledge, within their respective departments and schools.

>>ENDNOTES

1 > The concept for the "Tunnel of Oppression" as a pedagogical tool to engage students in understanding diversity and oppression began at Western Illinois State University in 1994. The program, recognized by the National Association of College and University Residence Halls in 1995 as "Program of the Year," has spread across the country to numerous college campuses including Syracuse University. It has been seen as a powerful and popular educational experience for college students. Students who participate in the program walk through "the tunnel" in groups of 6-8 people and view scenes depicting racism, sexism, homophobia, ableism, and religious oppression acted out by other students or via clips of a videotape. The 15 minute walk through the tunnel is followed by a facilitated discussion led by a staff member (often from Student Affairs/Residence Life). Organizers have seen this program as a method of engaging and educating students of non-minority groups about the experiences of members of oppressed groups. The program, however, has been called into question on campuses across the country; critics cite concerns about the shocking, emotional, and extreme nature of the scenes, such as depictions of a hate crime or a KKK gathering. Other concerns include the oversimplification of the complex and systemic issues related to oppression, as well as the de-contextualization of the issues depicted in the scenes. Critics argue that the experience is ineffective— allowing the viewer to remain distant and unable to make personal connections to the issues of oppression while depicting members of oppressed groups as powerless victims. The program has been conducted at Syracuse University since 2001.

LGBT Teaching Resources

PART III

Using Film Inclusively:
Or, Queering Your Class

Dean Allbritton

Films are fun. Most of us, when presented with the option of doing what's generally considered "real work" and watching a film, will unilaterally choose to plant ourselves in front of the screen, munch on a bit of popcorn, and absorb all the images and sounds. As teaching assistants, why should we be reluctant to capitalize on that willingness? In particular, and for the purposes of this book, we're speaking about opening minds to the varied experiences of the LGBT community. Nonetheless, teaching inclusively has nothing to do with forcing these views or creating cookie-cutter liberal students; rather, it allows for those ideologies not normally expressed or even accessible to the general student population to be given space in the classroom forum.

So the proposal here is that inclusive, effective, and responsible teaching practices can encourage students to question their surroundings and, at the same time, offer exposure to viewpoints quite different (or not so different) from their own. Problematic, however, is the inclusion of what is considered, for the most part, a very personal sphere—sexuality—into everyday classroom situations. This article doesn't propose a solution to that problem; the most that it can do is hold out three films that could be useful in launching these alternate ideas into the classroom and propelling rich discussions. Included are sample discussion questions that may serve as guidelines for beginning a dialogue within the classroom.

The three films discussed here are *Before Night Falls*, *Philadelphia,* and *Trembling Before G-d*. Out of the hundreds of informative and creative gay and lesbian-oriented films out there, these three were chosen for varied reasons: *Before Night Falls* is selected for its historical, political and literary emphases; *Philadelphia* is included for its focus on the legal politics of sexuality, as well as its emphasis on the AIDS epidemic; *Trembling before G-d* is included for its focus on religion, but also for its strong historical and political overtones, as it is a documentary of modern-day Israeli culture. These films are purposely diverse and contain topics and themes with multiple applications—greatly increasing the type of classrooms in which these films could be discussed.

For the arts and humanities class, the discussions that are suggested here may occur naturally, as open discussion is generally a built-in aspect of classroom practices. But for the math class, or geology class, where discussion isn't exactly on the list of things to do, the problem remains. Other articles within this book discuss aspects of incorporating awareness of sexual diversity and provide some suggestions for instructors in those disciplines. In addition, we all can take a lesson from these films that break from the familiar patterns of heteronormative thinking into more broadminded perspectives and ideas. Maybe the easiest and most effective way to introduce alternative ways of thinking and seeing—before showing the films or bending over backwards to incorporate unfamiliar and obtuse ideologies into your lesson plans—is to simply include the grain of these ideas into your presentation of the material.

For example, avoid homework assignments in which the student has to describe his girlfriend, or the female student needs to describe her boyfriend. What about the girl with a girlfriend, or the boy with a boyfriend? Does he change the pronouns? Why should she have to come out to her teacher? And is he self-defeating if he writes about some theoretical woman that could never exist for him? Thinking about how to consciously pay attention to these issues, even when they seem to have no real bearing on your life as a teaching assistant, is what I call "Teaching Inclusively 101."

The idea is to make this comfortable and natural for all involved. The great thing about using these films (or any others) in class is that they can easily spark a discussion that you may not feel comfortable enough trying to ignite on your own. And remember, the student that sees you struggle with being inclusive is going to be just as reluctant to think inclusively. Your job as a teaching assistant is to assist all students in the learning process, as diverse as they may be; opening up your mind and classroom to different streams of thought, regardless of your personal ideology, is one way to reach your students. Coating these ideas with an entertaining film is another way, softening the blow to more conservative ideologies and preparing students for the diversity of the world.

Before Night Falls

This film details the life of the late Reinaldo Arenas, an influential Cuban writer of various books and poems. Director Julian Schnabel retraces Arenas' origins in the rural Cuban countryside to his eventual development as a writer and self-exile in New York City. Arenas, played by Spanish actor Javier Bardem, suffers under the censorship and conservatism of the Castro regime and at the same time manages to smuggle some of his works out of the country for publication in France. Life in Castro's Cuba was difficult creatively as well as

>>discussion questions>>>>>>>>>>

Discuss the rise of the Castro regime. How does the movie treat these events?

In what ways is Reinaldo Arenas politically discriminated? Why?

Taking into account both the perspectives on the island as well as those exiled from the island, how is the United States portrayed in the film?

Read excerpts from Arenas' book *Before Night Falls*. In what ways does the text differ from the film version?

Read Arenas' suicide note. Why does he blame Castro for his death?

Arenas' work is noted for being somewhat autobiographical. Read some of Arenas' short stories and/or poems in conjunction with this film. How do we see autobiographical elements reflected in the story?

Does Arenas' position as a "storyteller" affect the veracity of his autobiography?

socially for Arenas, who was jailed several times for alleged sex charges. Finally in 1980 Arenas was allowed to leave Cuba for the United States, where he lived a lonely exile, sick with AIDS. This film was released in 2000, winning Best Actor and Grand Special Jury prizes at the Venice Film Festival and eventually garnering Javier Bardem with a Best Actor nomination at the 2001 Academy Awards (Hastings, 2004).

What other notable Cuban literary figures appear in the movie?

How does Arenas' sickness affect his life? His work?

Arenas says that he would not have contracted HIV had he been in Cuba. What do you think about this statement?

Consider and discuss the ways that sexuality intersects with religion, gender, nationality, politics and (dis)ability as represented in this film.

Philadelphia

When it premiered in 1993, *Philadelphia*, directed by Jonathan Demme, was the first big-budget Hollywood film to tackle the medical, political and social issues of AIDS. Playing lawyer and gay man Andrew Becket, Tom Hanks shines in his first Academy Award-winning performance. Andrew has recently contracted AIDS and fears the repercussions of disclosing his sickness. He is assigned a case involving the firm's most important client, but as AIDS-related lesions begin showing on his face, he is abruptly removed from the case and fired from the firm. Believing he has been discriminated against—fired due to his

Since the film's release a decade ago, what, if any, legal advancements have been made against AIDS discrimination in the workplace?

Do you feel that the mainstream voicing of AIDS, evident through this film and through Bruce Springsteen's accompanying song "Streets of Philadelphia," affects public awareness? In what ways is this positive? In what ways is this negative?

146

illness—Andrew decides to fight the firm in court; however, due to the firm's reputation, no lawyer in Philadelphia will commit to the case. Desperately, Andrew hires Joe Miller (Denzel Washington), a Black lawyer. Although Miller is homophobic, he agrees to take the case for the considerable monetary benefits as well as the exposure it will bring. As he begins working with Andrew, however, Miller comes to realize that the discrimination practiced against Andrew is very similar to the discrimination he himself battles daily (Brenner, 2004).

<<discussion questions<<

Do you think that this movie could be made in 2004? Why? In what ways would it be different?

Do a bit of research on the AIDS crisis and the early reaction of the U.S. government. What were some of the prevalent attitudes? How are the repercussions of these attitudes seen in the film?

This film, although groundbreaking at its time, represents a certain segment of the gay population and excludes others. How would the story be different if the main character were an African-American lesbian living with AIDS?

Do you think the film's portrayal of AIDS is accurate? Why or why not?

Do you believe Andrew had an obligation to tell his firm about his illness? Why or why not?

Do you think Andrew would have been discriminated against if he had been a heterosexual man with AIDS?

Research some of the reactions to this film. What was the social impact of its message? What was the public response to the film and why do you think the public reacted as it did?

Trembling before G-d

Making his feature-length film debut, director Sandi Samcha documents the lives of gays and lesbians in Hasidic and Orthodox Judaism in *Trembling before G-d*. Filmed in various locations, including New York, California, Florida, Israel and Britain, the

Many of the participants in the film are from large, urban areas. How would these perspectives be different in a more rural or an isolated community?

Pick someone from the documentary and trace his or her personal history. How is his or her perspective different from that of others in the film? Why do you think this is?

What are some of the basic tenets of Hasidic and Orthodox Judaism, according to the film? How is this different from the more liberal forms of Judaism?

What is the response of other forms of Judaism to the issue of homosexuality?

In general, what is the relationship between sexuality and other religions that you know?

Considering the history of social discrimination of the Jewish, how different do you think the experiences of a gay or lesbian Jewish person would be? How might their sexual identity complicate their religious oppression?

Does the film attempt to tackle historical issues of Judaism? In what ways?

Why is the film titled *Trembling before G-d*? Do some of the participants in the film have different views of who, or what, God is? Where do these differences come from?

film documents the lives of several people attempting to come to grips with the disparities between their faith and their sexuality. The audience meets pianist David, Los Angeles resident and Orthodox gay man, who has lived through over ten years of sexual therapy to "cure" him of his homosexuality. Michelle, a Hasidic lesbian in Brooklyn, has been shunned by her community since her divorce and coming out. Israel, also living in Brooklyn, is a gay man who has turned his back on his Hasidic life, distancing himself equally from his family for over 20 years. Some of the participants, however, prefer their anonymity due to their continued close involvement with the Hasidic and Orthodox community. Also included in this film is footage of various doctors and religious leaders discussing for and against the fusion of religion and sexual differences (LeVasseur, 2004).

Some of the participants of the film prefer to remain anonymous, while others freely show their faces, names and locations. Considering the possible repercussions within your community as well as issues of your own pride and self-worth, what would you have done? Why?

Film Suggestions[1]

After Stonewall (1999), historical documentary

All about my mother (*Todo sobre mi madre*) (1999), transgender identities, Spanish
    language

All Over the Guy (2001), gay identities, romantic comedy

And the Band played On (1993), dramatization of the Emerging AIDS epidemic, AIDS
    studies, American history, American politics

Before Night Falls (Antes que anochezca) (2001), Cuban politics, Cuban literature,
    Spanish language

Before Stonewall (1984), historical documentary

Bent (1997), German history, Global politics, Holocaust

Better Than Chocolate (1999), romantic comedy, lesbians

Big Eden (2000), gay-related romantic comedy

The Birdcage (1996), comedy, gay parenting, non-traditional families

The Birdcage (La Cage Aux Folles) (1979), male sexual identity, French language, gay
    parenting

Bound (1996), lesbian identity, thriller

Boys' Life (3 parts) (1995), gay identity, college, coming out

Boys Don't Cry (1999), Transgender identity and experiences, hate crimes, based on a
    true story

Brandon Teena Story (1998), transgender identity and experiences, hate crimes,
    documentary

But I'm a Cheerleader (1999), Lesbian identity, comedy

The Celluloid Closet (1996), documentary on the history of LGBT identities in
    Hollywood films

CONTINUED>>

Chutney Popcorn (2000), lesbian identity, cultural differences
Come Undone (Presque Rien) (2000), gay identity, coming out, French language
Defying Gravity (1997), college campus, fraternities, coming out
Desert Hearts (1985), coming out, lesbian identity
Eight Women (8 Femmes) (2002), lesbian identity, camp, French language
Fire (1996), lesbian identity, marriage issues in India
Frida (2002), bisexual themes
Gia (1998), lesbian identity
Go Fish (1994), lesbian communities
Hedwig and the Angry Inch (2001), Transgender studies
The Hours (2003), lesbian identity, English Literature, AIDS
If These Walls Could Talk 2 (2000), lesbian couples, three dramatic short films
Incredibly True Story of Two Girls in Love (1995), lesbian romantic comedy
It's Elementary (1996), gay issues and schooling, documentary
Kissing Jessica Stein (2001), Queer studies, lesbian identities, romantic comedy
The Laramie Project (2002), Matthew Shepard hate crime, documentary style
Ma Vie en Rose (1997), transgender/male sexual identity, French language
My Beautiful Launderette (1986), English history, hate crimes, discrimination, interracial
     issues
The Next Best Thing (2000), non-traditional families, comedy
Nico and Dani (Krámpadk) (2000), coming of age, gay identity, Spanish language
Normal (2003), Transgender studies, families
Out of the Past: the struggle for gay and lesbian rights in America (1998), American
     history, sexual identity
Paragraph 175 (2000), German history, Global politics, Holocaust
Paris is Burning (1990), documentary on drag shows by men of color in Harlem, voguing
Parting Glances (1986), AIDS studies, American history
Philadelphia (1993), AIDS studies, American history, Law
Southern Comfort (2001), transgender love story, documentary
Stonewall (1996), American history, sexual identity
The Times of Harvey Milk (1984), gay politics, American history, hate crimes,
     documentary
Tongues Untied (1990), African-American studies, gay identity, masculinity
Trembling before G-d (2001), Jewish history, Global politics, religion, sexuality

Trick (1999), comedy, gay romance
The Vagina Monologues (2002), theatre
performances, sexuality
The Watermelon Woman (1996), lesbian
identity, African-American
studies
Wilde (1998), English history, English
Literature, male sexual identity

<<link ed <<<<<<<<<<<<<<
For more information on LGBT
films, visit >>

www.glaad.org
www.gay-films.net

>>REFERENCES

Brenner, P. Philadelphia. Retrieved 2004 from All Movie Guide at
http://www.allmovie.com
Hastings, M. Before Night Falls. Retrieved 2004 from All Movie Guide at
http://www.allmovie.com
Le Vasseur, A. Trembling before G-d. Retrieved 2004 from All Movie Guide at
http://www.allmovie.com

>>ENDNOTES

1 > Special thanks to the LGBT Resource Center at Syracuse University for their
incredible contribution to this list of LGBT films. In fact, most of these films are
available for loan from the Resource Center. For more information on the Center,
visit their website at http://students.syr.edu/lgbt.

>>campus resources

LGBT Resource Center
315-443-3983

Email: aljaehni@syr.edu
Online: http://students.syr.edu/lgbt
750 Ostrom Avenue, Syracuse, NY

The LGBT Resource Center provides trainings & educational presentations; sponsors various lectures and programs; offers support and discussion groups; maintains a current and diverse resource library that consists of movies, educational videos, magazines, newspapers, and books; provides a safe space and information to LGBT students, faculty, and staff at Syracuse University.

The University Senate Committee on LGBT Concerns

Formed in 2002, it strives to improve the campus climate for LGBT faculty, staff and students. Through two Vision Fund Grants, the Senate Committee has sponsored and co-sponsored numerous events on campus, including the Transgender Teach-In and an upcoming conference on LGBT Studies. Please contact Margaret Himley (Arts & Sciences) at mrhimley@syr.edu or Andrew London (Sociology) at aslondon@syr.edu for more information.

>>discussion groups>>

Planet Orange

> Planet Orange is a drop-in group for LGBTQ students that meets every Monday from 7-9 p.m. at the LGBT Resource Center. Topics vary from week to week, with a social event the last Monday of every month.

identities (n) motion

> identities (n) motion is a confidential discussion group for students who are seeking support or who have questions about their sexuality that meets every week. Sponsored by the Counseling Center and the LGBT Resource Center.

For more information, contact the LGBT Resource Center at 443-3983.

153

Delta Lambda Phi

315-443-1529

Email: syracuse@dlp.org
Online: http://dlp.org/syracolony

Delta Lambda Phi is a national fraternity founded by gay men for all men. DLP's purpose is to enhance the quality of life among gay, bisexual, and progressive men by providing dignified and purposeful social, service and recreational activities.

Fusion

315-443-3983

Fusion creates space for LGBT people of color to bring all of who they are together...to network, socialize, talk about their backgrounds, and make sense of their experiences within LGBT communities and their cultural/ethnic communities. Open to students, staff, and faculty. Meeting times to be determined at the start of each Fall semester.

Open Doors

315-443-1529

Email: suopendoors@yahoo.com
Online: http://students.syr.edu/opendoors

The LGBTQA graduate student organization meets biweekly at the LGBT Resource Center. The meetings consist of discussions concerning LGBT concerns, issues, as well as upcoming events. The group sponsors programming throughout the year to address LGBT students, including an annual film festival entitled Reel Queer. Meeting times to be determined at the start of each Fall semester.

>>student organizations

OutLaw: Gay/Straight Law Student Alliance
315-443-1962

Email: wrpruitt@syr.edu
Online: http://www.law.syr.edu/students/organizations/lambda/

The Gay/Straight Law Student Alliance promotes awareness and understanding of issues associated with sexual diversity and the law through education and scholarship. OutLaw advocates acceptance and inclusion of all forms of sexual diversity in the law through political and legal activism. OutLaw supports all segments of the Syracuse community by being a safe space within the Syracuse University College of Law.

Pride Union
315-443-1529

Email: suprideunion@yahoo.com
Online: http://students.syr.edu/prideunion

LGBTQA undergraduate student organization that meets every Wednesday at 9 p.m. at the LGBT Resource Center. The group sponsors programming that advocates and educates people about LGBT concerns. Pride Union is a central participant in planning Coming Out Week events, as well as the annual drag show and competition.

Compiled by Justin Welch

CNY Polyamory Network
Email: CNYPoly@yahoo.com
Online: http://www.geocities.com/cnypoly
or http://clubs.yahoo.com/clubs/cnypolyamory

Serves Syracuse and surrounding areas by providing support to people who are interested in having multiple loving relationships at the same time.

Coalition for Lesbian Visibility
315-568-9364
PO Box 517, Seneca Falls, NY 13148

Diverse group of women who hold monthly dinners and socials in the Finger Lakes area, usually on the second Saturday of each month.

Expressing Our Nature (EON)
315-426-1658
Online: http://www.nytga.org/eon/

Serves the transgender community of upstate New York. Call for meeting times and locations.

Gay Friendship Network
Garrett: 315-476-3704 or Kevin: 315-428-0806
326 Montgomery St., Syracuse, NY

A community organization that holds meetings on the 2nd and 4th Monday of every month at 7:30 p.m. The Network offers a setting for people to meet new friends and gain support.

GRADS Guys Responding And Demanding Safety
315-475-2430, 1-800-475-2437
Email: REACHGRADS@juno.com
627 West Genesee Street, Syracuse, NY 13204

GRADS serves as an advocacy and support group for men. They offer discussion groups, as well as programs and workshops dealing with HIV/AIDS, sex, and intimacy.

Journeymen, Ltd.
Online: http://journeymenltd.com
PO Box 1761, Syracuse, NY 132001-1761

A social group for gay men interested in motorcycles and leather. They hold a bar night on the 4th Saturday of each month starting at 10 p.m. at Spirits Tavern, 205 N. West St., Syracuse, NY.

OUTWords!
315-476-6582
Online: http://www.outwordscny.com
709 E. Genesee St., Syracuse, NY 13210

A monthly publication and website that covers current LGBT issues and events. It also provides a listing of local resources for LGBT people.

Pride Community Center of Central NY
315-426-1650
Email: PrideSyr@aol.com
709 East Genesee Street, Syracuse, NY

This center sponsors and provides programming to educate people in the Central New York area about LGBT concerns.

Safer Community Project
315-475-2430
Email: glbtyouth@aidscommunityresources.com

Provides social support for LGBT and questioning people ages 14 to 20. The Project also offers support to parents and provides LGBT-sensitivity workshops.

SAGE Senior Action in a Gay Environment
315-478-1923
Email: sageupstate@yahoo.com
Online: http://www.geocities.com/sageupstate
PO Box 6271, Syracuse, NY 13217

SAGE offers support and activities to older LGBT people in the CNY area. Meetings are held monthly. Call for more information.

The Stonewall Committee
315-476-6226
246 E. Water St., Syracuse, NY 13202

An advocacy and support organization that holds and sponsors programs concerning LGBT issues/concerns. Call for more information.

Syracuse Gay & Lesbian Chorus
315-476-4329
Email: sglc@swns.net

Congregational Church, 232 East Onondaga St., Syracuse, NY The chorus holds private and public concerts, as well as sponsoring musical events. Auditions are held in the fall and the beginning of each calendar year.

Syracuse Men's Club

Online: http://www.geocities.com/WestHollywood/4200/
SMC_Home.htm
PO Box 3460, Syracuse, NY 13220

Social group for men interested in leather or S&M or consider
themselves to be bears. A bar night is held on the 4th Friday
of each month at Spirits Tavern, 205 N. West St., Syracuse,
NY.

Women's Information Center

315-478-4636
Online: http://womensinfo.tripod.com/
601 Allen St., Syracuse, NY 13210

A non-profit organization that promotes feminist principles of
empowering women regardless of their race, ethnicity, sexual
orientation, disability, or economic status.

Youth Group

Email: glbtyouth@aidscommunityresources.com
627 W. Genesee St, Syracuse, NY

Support group for gay, lesbian, bisexual, and questioning youth,
ages 14 to 20. Meetings are held every Thursday from 7-8:30
p.m.

AIDS Community Resources

315-475-2430 or 1-888-475-2437 or 1-800-475-2430
Online: www.aidscommunityresources.com
627 West Genesee St., Syracuse, NY 13204

Through programming and sponsored groups, this organization aims to prevent the spread of HIV infection, increase the quality of life for HIV positive people, as well as educating people about sexually transmitted infections.

American Indian Community House HIV/AIDS Project

315-478-3767

The project serves to develop culturally relevant outreach, education, and case management services to Native American communities in New York.

Anonymous HIV Testing

1-800-562-9423

Provides HIV information, referrals, and how to obtain a free HIV test anonymously

CNY Center for Excellence

315-464-5533

The center provides HIV treatment, testing, and counseling.

CNY HIV Care Network

315-472-8099
701 Erie Blvd. West, Syracuse, NY 13204

Network provides information sharing and program coordination for HIV/ AIDS programs, advocates, and people living with HIV/AIDS.

>>HIV/AIDS services

DePalmer House

315-475-1544
PO Box 690, Syracuse, NY 13201

Transitional housing for people with HIV/AIDS who are also homeless or housing vulnerable.

FACES, Southwest Community Center

315-474-6823
401 South Ave., Syracuse, NY 13204

Provides education concerning HIV/AIDS to Syracuse residents, with an emphasis on people of color.

Friends of Dorothy

315-471-6851
PO Box 264, Syracuse, NY 13208

Provides care and housing for people living with HIV/AIDS. A dinner is held monthly for anyone wishing to attend. Call for more information.

Hospice of CNY

315-634-1100
990 Seventh North St., Liverpool, NY 13088

The Names Project of Syracuse

315-498-4940
670 S. Salina St., Nedrow, NY 13120

Project provides showings of panels from the AIDS Memorial Quilt.

Central New York Chapter - New York Civil Liberties Union
315-471-2821 / Fax 315-471-1077
2100 E. Genesee St., Syracuse, NY 13210

Organization works through political and legal action to protect American citizens' civil liberties.

CNY Diversity
315-476-6626
246 E. Water St., Syracuse, NY 13202-1122

Group engages in direct action on behalf of major party candidates that are responsive to LGBT people.

Empire State Pride Agenda
Online: http://www.prideagenda.org
716-271-2420, Fax 716-271-0216
274 Goodman St N. #C269-32, Rochester, NY 14607-1154

Nation's largest statewide organization for LGBT civil rights and is committed to achieving full equality for LGBT people.

National Organization for Women, Greater Syracuse Chapter
315-446-7823
201 Ambergate Rd., Dewitt, NY 13214

NOW is the nation's largest group of feminist activists. The group works to bring full equality to women.

>>political action

First Unitarian Universalist Society of Syracuse
315-446-5940
Email: Firstuusyr@aol.com
Online: http://home.twcny.rr.com/firstuusyr/index.html
250 Waring Rd., Syracuse, NY 13224

Their congregation is open to the full participation and development of LGBT people.

Plymouth Church
315-474-4836
232 E. Onondaga St., Syracuse, NY 13202

Church is the meeting site for the Syracuse Gay & Lesbian Chorus; the chorus often performs there.

Ray of Hope Church
315-471-6618; 1-800-367-1463
Online: http://www.rayofhopechurch.com

Offers worship to LGBT people on Wednesday nights at 6 p.m. at the May Memorial Unitarian Universalist Building, 3800 E. Genessee St., Syracuse, NY.

Syracuse Gay/Lesbian Catholics & Friends
315-636-7726
Email: saintaelred@yahoo.com

The group holds a meeting on the 1st and 3rdSunday of each month at St. Andrew's Catholic Church, 124 Alden St., Syracuse, NY. They meet for dinners, liturgy, reception of the sacrament and worship.

religious groups

Charades

315-475-3000
Online: http://charades.cc/
West Fayette Street, Syracuse, NY

Open Thursday to Saturday 8 p.m.-2 a.m.; Friday Happy Hour at 4 p.m.; Sunday 3 p.m.-2 a.m. The club is open to 18 and over Thursday through Sunday, otherwise it's open only to patrons over 21. Open to LGBT people, it features drag performances and a range of music for dancing.

Club 950

315-425-1450
Online: http://www.club950.com/950/index1.htm
950 Spencer Street, Syracuse, NY

Open Wednesday through Saturday from 10 p.m. – 2 a.m. The bar/club is open to women age 21 and over.

Rain Lounge

315-474-3487
218 N. Franklin St., Syracuse, NY

Open Monday through Saturday until 2 a.m. It serves mainly as a bar/ hangout for gay men.

Spirits Tavern

315- 471-9279
Online: http://www.spiritstavern.com/
205 N. West Street, Syracuse, NY

Open daily until 2 a.m. Serves as a bar/hangout. Drag shows and strippers are often featured. Pride Kitchen is scheduled weekly, call for times.

>>bars/clubs

Trexx

315-474-6408
Online: http://www.trexxonline.com/
323 N Clinton Street, Syracuse, NY

Open Wednesday through Sunday nights until 4 a.m. Anyone 18 and over is welcome. The dance and video bar, which is open to straight and LGBT people, usually provides techno/house music.

Compiled by Justin Welch

>>online resources

>Annotated Links to LGBT/Queer Studies Resources
http://www.uic.edu/depts/quic/resources/lgbt_studies.html

This rich directory includes descriptions and links to: Directories of College/ University-based LGBT Scholars, Programs & Resources; Queer Studies Resources; National LGBT Centers and Institutions; LGBT Libraries and Archives; Professional Caucuses/Organizations; Journals/Periodicals/ Literary Publications; as well as other sites of potential interest.

> Center for Lesbian and Gay Studies (CLAGS)
http://web.gc.cuny.edu/clags/online.htm

CLAGS website contains a wide range of information for any academic interested in scholarly LGBT content. This website features a searchable online directory of LGBTQ Studies sources, including related programs, conferences, workshops, and scholars. Click on "Links" to find a broad menu of resources, such as Academic Resources (including syllabi with LGBT content, Funding Sources, Think Tanks & Policy Resources); General Resources with links including Queer Theory and LGBT Research Centers; Professional Caucuses/Organizations; Mailing Lists; Calls for Papers; and a broad list of LGBT political groups and organizations.

>LGBT/Queer Studies Websites
http://www.public.iastate.edu/~savega/les_biga.htm

This extensive directory, organized by Susan A. Vega Garcia, includes selected LGBT web resources useful for academic research and information purposes. Garcia evaluated all recommended websites for breadth, perceived authority, stability, usefulness, and accuracy. Directory includes LGBT-related web index sites, clearinghouses, and directories (sites that gather or point to additional resources), e-journals, and electronic news (all which include actual content).

>National and International Gay and Lesbian Organizations and Publications
http://faculty.washington.edu/alvin/gayorg.htm

This website, organized by Alvin Fritz of the University of Washington Libraries, contains 47 pages of non-profit and information-providing organizations and publications with reasonably up-to-date websites having numerous full-text resources and links to many LGBT topics, including bookstores/video stores, religion/spirituality, business, education, and sports/social/recreation/travel.

>Resources Related to Lesbian, Gay, Bisexual, and Transgender Issues
http://student.ccbcmd.edu/~gweight/lgbt/

This resource guide contains links to many "general" LGBT organizations, as well as additional information on academic/educational resources and other sites with content specifically dedicated to information for/about lesbians, gay men, bisexual, and transgender people.

>ACT UP/New York
http://www.actupny.org/

ACT UP is a diverse, non-partisan group of individuals united in anger and committed to direct action to end the AIDS crisis.

>Families-Like-Mine, Learning about the Transgender Community
http://www.familieslikemine.com/insight/transphobia.html

Families Like Mine is a web site dedicated to decreasing isolation for people who have parents who are lesbian, gay, bisexual, or transgender (LGBT), and bringing voice to the experiences of these families. Among the links on this website is a short article entitled, "Learning about the transgender community." However, you should also investigate the other resources this website offers.

>Gender Identity 101: A Transgender Primer
http://www.sagatucson.org/tgnetaz/gender_101.htm

This is an excellent website that introduces readers to gender and transgender topics, issues, and resources.

>GenderPac
http://www.gpac.org/

The Gender Public Advocacy Coalition (GenderPAC) works to end discrimination and violence caused by gender stereotypes by changing public attitudes, educating elected officials, and expanding legal rights. GenderPAC also promotes understanding of the connection between discrimination based on gender stereotypes and sex, sexual orientation, age, race, and class.

>Gay and Lesbian Alliance Against Defamation (GLAAD)

http://www.glaad.org

GLAAD is dedicated to promoting and ensuring fair, accurate, and inclusive representation of individuals and events in all media as a means of eliminating homophobia and discrimination based on gender identity and sexual orientation.

>Human Rights Campaign (HRC)

http://www.hrc.org/

The HRC is a national organization working for lesbian, gay, bisexual, and transgender equal rights. This website is valuable if you're looking for information on LGBT legislation, including facts and figures.

>International Journal of Transgenderism

http://www.symposion.com/ijt/index.htm

This is a free online journal with links to full text articles on an extensive number of transgender-related articles. If you're looking for articles to include in classroom content, you're likely to find something useful here.

>Lambda Legal Defense and Education Fund

http://www.lambdalegal.org/cgi-bin/iowa/about

Lambda Legal is a national organization committed to achieving full recognition of the civil rights of lesbians, gay men, bisexuals, the transgendered, and people with HIV or AIDS through impact litigation, education, and public policy work.

>National Gay and Lesbian Task Force (NGLTF)
http://www.thetaskforce.org./citemap.cfm

NGLTF is a national progressive organization working for the civil rights of gay, lesbian, bisexual, and transgender people. This website contains information on a wide variety of LGBT issues including aging, families, hate crimes, military, religion, same sex marriage, and racial justice. This is a great site to visit if you're looking for facts and figures. Also, the NGLTF website contains an excellent directory of LGBT organizations.

>National Transgender Advocacy Coalition (NTAC)
http://www.ntac.org/

NTAC works for the advancement of understanding and the attainment of full civil rights for all transgendered, intersexed, and gender variant people in every aspect of society, and actively opposes discriminatory acts by all means legally available. This website contains information about legislation that is specifically related to the transgender community as well as facts and figures, including transgender death statistics.

>Parents, Families, and Friends of Lesbians and Gay Men (PFLAG)
http://www.pflag.org/

PFLAG promotes the health and well-being of gay, lesbian, bisexual, and transgendered persons, and their families and friends through: *support*, to cope with an adverse society; *education*, to enlighten an ill-informed public; and *advocacy*, to end discrimination and to secure equal civil rights. PFLAG provides opportunity for dialogue about sexual orientation and gender identity, and acts to create a society that is healthy and respectful of human diversity.

>Gayscape
http://www.jwpublishing.com/gayscape/classic.html

For 8 years Gayscape has specialized in LGBT content; contains over 102,000 indexed sites.

>Rainbowquery.com
http://www.rainbowquery.com

This keyword search engine claims to be "The largest, most complete GLBT search on the internet!" With subject headings as varied as Arts & Entertainment, Families, Health & Fitness, Government & Politics, Erotica, and Daily News, you'll be sure to find a vast array of LGBT-related information.

>>search engines

Compiled by Kathleen Farrell

Citations for Classroom and Other Campus-Related LGBT Texts

Adina Mulliken

Many of these materials are available online through Syracuse University Library's website or in print or microfilm in the Library. You are welcome to call Adina Mulliken, Reference Librarian, 443-9519, or Kelly Hovendick, Reference Librarian, 443-4807, if you would like help locating any these items.

This bibliography contains periodical articles and books that were published from 1995 to 2003. Please be aware that this is not a comprehensive bibliography on these topics. Brief descriptions are included for a few items when the title would otherwise be unclear. For space reasons, I have excluded most materials about LGBT- pedagogy in specific disciplines, such as literature and psychology; materials concerning LGBT-support offices; items that are geographically limited or specific to a type of institution such as community or religious colleges; materials about crimes and campus safety; and items that are about athletics, counseling or career development. Information about these and other related topics can be researched through the SU Library.

Sexuality and the Classroom (Teaching Resources)

Addressing homophobia and heterosexism on college campuses. (2003). *Family Therapy, 30* (2), 113.
   Description: Includes specific classroom techniques for handling homophobia and heterosexism; deals with academic freedom, diversity training, nontraditional families, and religion; includes a list of feature films, documentaries and more.

Cramer, E. P. (2002). *Addressing homophobia and heterosexism on college campuses.* Binghamton, NY: Harrington Park Press.

D'Augelli, A.R. (1992). Teaching lesbian/gay development: From oppression to exceptionality. *Journal of Homosexuality,* 22 (3-4), 213-227.

Doggette, A. L., Reid, J. D., Garfield, L. D., & Hoy, S. J. (2001, Winter). From curiosity to care: Heterosexual student interest in sexual diversity courses. *Teaching of Psychology, 28* (1), 21-26.

Evans, N. J. (2000, Summer). Creating a positive learning environment for gay, lesbian, and bisexual students. *New Directions for Teaching and Learning,* 2000 (82), 81-87.
   Description: Suggests ways faculty can improve the learning environment for GLB students, especially because these students often first acknowledge their sexual orientation in college.

Foster, D. W. (Winter, 2002). Cultural studies and sexual ideologies. *ADFL Bulletin,* 33 (2), 20-24.

Green, B. C. (1998, September). Thinking about students who do not identify as gay, lesbian, or bisexual, but. . . *Journal of American College Health, 47* (2), 89-91.

Husted, B. L. (2001, November). Hope, for the dry side. *College English, 64* (2), 243-49.
   Description: Discusses a writing class and the teacher's attempts to address students' racism, homophobia, and distrust of their own skills in writing.

Kopelson, K. (2002, September). Dis/Integrating the gay/queer binary: "Reconstructed identity politics" for a performative pedagogy. *College English, 65* (1), 17-35.

Levesque, P. J. (2000). *Promoting communication: Teaching tolerance of homosexual persons while addressing religious fears.* California. (ERIC Document Reproduction Service No. ED453702).

Lopez, G. & Chism, N. (1993, Summer). Classroom concerns of gay and lesbian students: The invisible minority. *College Teaching, 41*(3), 97-103.

Magee, D. B. (1998). *Contact and comfort zones: Gay male praxis in the composition classroom.* Texas. (ERIC Document Reproduction Service No. ED422577).

Mayberry, K. J. (1996). *Teaching what you're not: Identity politics in higher education.* New York: New York University Press.

Ottenritter, N. (1998, April). The courage to care: Addressing sexual minority issues on campus. In: *Removing vestiges,* No.1, 13-20. Washington, DC: American Association of Community Colleges. (ERIC Document Reproduction Service No. ED438013).

Rabow, J., Stein, J. M., & Conley, T. D. (1999, June). Teaching social justice and encountering society: The pink triangle experiment. *Youth & Society, 30* (4), 483-514.

Description: Students wore pink triangles and shared their thoughts about the stigmatizing experience.

Renn, K. A. (2000, Fall). Including all voices in the classroom: Teaching lesbian, gay, and bisexual students. *College Teaching, 48* (4), 129-35.

Sanlo, R. L. (1998). *Working with lesbian, gay, bisexual, and transgender college students: A handbook for faculty and administrators.* Westport, CT: Greenwood Press.

Tierney, W. G. (1993, Summer). Academic freedom and the parameters of knowledge. *Harvard Educational Review, 63* (2), 143-160.

Vandrick, S. (2001, February 28). *Teaching sexual issues in ESL classes.* California. (ERIC Document Reproduction Service No. ED474464).

Van Puymbroeck, C. M. (2001). The mentoring web: A model to increase retention of lesbian, gay, and bisexual undergraduates. College Park, MD: University of Maryland Counseling Center. (ERIC Document Reproduction Service No. ED456716).

Coming Out in the Classroom/Being Out on Campus as an Instructor

Allen, K. R. (1995, April). Opening the classroom closet: Sexual orientation and self-disclosure. *Family Relations: Journal of Applied Family & Child Studies, 44* (2), 136-141.

175

Coming out in class: Disclosure of sexual orientation and teaching evaluations. (1997, February). *Teaching of Psychology, 24* (1), 32-35.

Griffin, P. (1992). From hiding out to coming out: Empowering lesbian and gay educators. In K. M. Harbeck (Ed.), *Coming out of the classroom closet: Gay and lesbian students, teachers, and curricula* (pp. 167-196). New York: Harrington Park Press.

The institutional climate for lesbian, gay and bisexual education faculty: What is the pivotal frame of reference? (2002). *Journal of Homosexuality, 43* (1), 11-37.

Lamb, M. R. (1998). *Passing as teacher: Constructing a lesbian feminist pedagogy.* Texas. (ERIC Document Reproduction Service No. ED422587).

Mahaffey, C. J. (1999, May). *The rhetoric of coming out and its effect on lesbian and gay teachers: Gay identity politics in the public sphere and in private lives.* [An Annotated Bibliography.] (ERIC Document Reproduction Service No. ED467427).

Myrick, R. & Brown, M.H. (1998, October). Out of the closet and into the classroom: A survey of lesbian, gay, and bisexual educators' classroom strategies and experiences in colleges and universities. *Journal of Gay, Lesbian, & Bisexual Identity, 3* (4), 295-317.

Rofes, E. (2000, November). Bound and gagged: Sexual silences, gender conformity, and the gay male teacher. *Sexualities, 3* (4), 439-462.

Russ, T. L. & Hunt, S. K. (2002, July). Coming out in the classroom... an occupational hazard? The influence of sexual orientation on teacher credibility and perceived student learning. *Communication Education, 51* (3), 311-324.

Skelton, A. (2000, Spring). 'Camping it up to make them laugh?' Gay men teaching in higher education. *Teaching in Higher Education, 5* (2), 181-93.

Talburt, S. (2000). *Subject to identity: Knowledge, sexuality, and academic practices in higher education.* New York: SUNY Series, Identities in the Classroom. (ERIC Document Reproduction Service No. ED441368).

Wallace, D. L. (2002, September). Out in the Academy: Heterosexism, invisibility, and double consciousness. *College English, 65* (1), 53-66.

Woods, S. E., & Harbeck, K. M. (1991). Living in two worlds: The identity management strategies used by lesbian physical educators. *Journal of Homosexuality*, 22, 141-166.

Campus Climate and LGBT College Students

Attitudes toward gay, lesbian and bisexual persons among heterosexual liberal arts college students. (2002). *Journal of Homosexuality, 43* (1), 61-84.

Evans, N. J. (2001). The experiences of lesbian, gay, and bisexual youths in university communities. In A. R. D'Augelli & C. J. Patterson (Eds.), *Lesbian, gay, and bisexual Identities and youth: Psychological perspectives,* 181-98. London: Oxford University Press.

Guth, L. J., Hewitt-Gervais, C., Smith, S., & Fisher, M. S. (2000, September-October). Student attitudes toward AIDS and homosexuality: The effects of a speaker with HIV. *Journal of College Student Development, 41* (5), 503-12.

Howard, K. & Stevens, A. (Eds.). (2000). *Out & about on campus: Personal accounts by lesbian, gay, bisexual, & transgendered college students.* Los Angeles: Alyson Publications.

Mohr, J. J. & Sedlacek, W. E. (2000, January-February). Perceived barriers to friendship with lesbians and gay men among university students. *Journal of College Student Development, 41* (1), 70-80.

Lesbian, gay, bisexual, and transgender college students with disabilities: A look at multiple cultural minorities. (2002, September). *Psychology in the Schools, 39* (5), 525-38.

Renn, K. A. & Bilodeau, B. (2002, November 22). *Queer student leaders: A case study of leadership development and lesbian, gay, bisexual, and transgender student involvement.* (ERIC Document Reproduction Service No. ED470048).

Sanlo, R. (2000, November-December). Lavender graduation: Acknowledging the lives and achievement of lesbian, gay, bisexual, and transgender college students. *Journal of College Student Development, 41* (6), 643-47.

Schulte, L. J. (2002). Similarities and differences in homophobia among African Americans versus Caucasians. *Race, Gender & Class, 9* (4), 71-93.

Sexual attitudes among Hispanic college students: Differences between males and females. (2003). *International Journal of Adolescence & Youth, 11*(1), 79-89.

Shepard, C. F., Yeskel, F., & Outcalt, C. (1995). Lesbian, gay, bisexual, and transgender campus organizing: A comprehensive manual. New York: National Gay and Lesbian Task Force. (ERIC Document Reproduction Service No. ED449723).

>>academic resources
related to sexuality
and gender studies

Abelove, H., Barale, M.A., & Halperin, D.M. (Eds.). (1993). *The lesbian and gay studies reader.* New York: Routledge.

Arguelles, L. & Rich, B.R. (1989). Homosexuality, homophobia, and revolution: Notes toward an understanding of the Cuban lesbian and gay male experience. In Duberman, Vicinus, & Chauncey (Eds.), *Hidden from history,* 441-55. New York: New American Library.

Bloom, A. (1994, July 18). The body lies. *The New Yorker,* 38-44, 46-49.

Bornstein, K. (1994). *Gender outlaw: On men, women, and the rest of us.* New York: Vintage Books.

Boykin, K. (1996). *One more river to cross: Black and gay in America.* New York: Anchor Books.

Butler, J. (1990). *Gender trouble.* New York: Routledge.

Califia, P. (1997). *Sex changes: The politics of transgenderism.* San Francisco: Cleis Press.

Carrier, J.M. (1985). Mexican male bisexuality. In F. Klein and T.J. Wolf (Eds.), *Two lives to lead: Bisexuality in men and women,* 75-85. New York: Harrington.

Chauncey, G. (1994). *Gay New York.* New York: Basic Books.

Cromwell, J. (1999). *Transmen and ftms: Identities, bodies, genders, and sexualities.* Urbana, IL: University of Illinois Press.

Cruz-Malavé, A. & Manalansan, M.F. (Eds.). (2002). *Queer globalizations: Citizenship and the afterlife of colonialism.* New York: New York University Press.

D'Emilio, J. & Freedman, E. (1988). *Intimate matters: A history of sexuality in America.* NY: Harper and Row.

Duggan, L. (1992). Making it perfectly queer. *Socialist Review, 22* (1), 11-31.

179

Fausto-Sterling, A. (1993). The five sexes: Why male and female are not enough. *The Sciences*, March/April, 20-24.

Feinberg, L. (1996). *Transgender warriors: Making history from Joan of Arc to RuPaul.* Boston: Beacon Press.

Foucault, M. (1980). *The history of sexuality: An introduction.* New York: Vintage.

Freedman, E. (1995). The historical construction of homosexuality in the US. *Socialist Review, 25* (1), 31-46.

Fuss, D. (Ed.). (1991). *Inside/out: Lesbian theories, gay theories.* New York: Routledge.

Glick, E., Garber, L., Holland, S., Balderston, D., & Quiroga, J. (2003). New directions in multiethnic, racial, and global queer studies. *GLQ, 10* (1), 123-137.

Gross, L. & Woods, J.D. (Eds.). (1999). *The Columbia reader on lesbians and gay men in media, society and politics.* New York: Columbia University Press.

Halberstam, J. (1998). *Female masculinities.* Durham, NC: Duke University Press.

Hubbard, R. (1995). The social construction of sexuality. In P. Rothenberg (Ed.), *Race, class, and gender in the United States.* New York: St. Martin's Press.

Katz, J. (1990). The invention of heterosexuality. *Socialist Review, 20*, 7-34.

Kessler, S. (1990). The medical construction of gender: Case management of intersexed infants. *Signs, 16*, 3-26.

Laumann, E.O., Gagnon, J.H., Michael, R.T., & Michaels, S. (1994). *The social organization of sexuality: Sexual practices in the United States.* Chicago: University of Chicago Press.

Leong, R. (Ed.). (1996). *Asian American sexualities: Dimensions of the gay and lesbian experience.* New York: Routledge.

Lorber, J. (1996). Beyond the binaries: Depolarizing the categories of sex, sexuality, and gender. *Sociological Inquiry, 66* (2), 143-159.

Miller, N. (1992). *Out in the world: Gay and lesbian life from Buenos Aires to Bangkok.* New York: Random House.

Moraga, C. & Anzaldua. (Eds.). (1983). *This bridge called my back: Writings by radical women of color.* New York: Kitchen Table, Women of Color Press.

Morton, D. (Ed.). (1996). *The material queer: A lesbigay cultural studies reader.* Boulder, CO: Westview.

Murray, S. (1996). *American gay.* Chicago: University of Chicago Press.

Nardi, P.M. & Schneider, B.E. (Eds.). (1998). *Social Perspectives in Lesbian and Gay Studies: A Reader.* London and New York: Routledge.

Ratti, R. (Ed.). (1993). *A lotus of another color: An unfolding of the South Asian gay and lesbian experience.* Boston: Alyson Publications.

Rodriguez Rust, P.C. (2000). *Bisexuality in the United States: A social science reader.* New York: Columbia University Press.

Sedgwick, E. (1990). *Epistemology of the closet.* Berkeley: University of California Press.

Seidman, S. (Ed.). (1996). *Queer theory/sociology.* Malden, MA: Blackwell.

Shapiro, J.P. (1993). *No pity: People with disabilities forging a new civil rights movement.* New York: Times Books.

Sexuality Information and Education Council of the Unites States. (1999). SIECUS Report. [Special volume on transgender issues]. Vol. 28, No.1.

Terry, J. (1999). *An American obsession: Science, medicine, and homosexuality.* Chicago and London: The University of Chicago Press.

Trujillo, C. (Ed.). (1991). *Chicana lesbians: The girls our mothers warned us about.* Berkeley: Third Woman Press.

Warner, M. (Ed.). (1993). *Fear of a queer planet: Queer politics and social theory.* Minneapolis, MN: University of Minnesota Press.

Weston, K. (1991). *Families we choose: Lesbians, gays, kinship.* New York: Columbia University Press.

Wilchins, R. A. (1997). *Read my lips: Sexual subversion and the end of gender.* Ithaca, NY: Firebrand Books.

Compiled by Kathleen Farrell

>>glossary
of LGBT-related terms

Ability: In this volume we intentionally substitute the word "ability" in place of the more common medical term "disability" in order to highlight differing physical and mental abilities as a range of variations in the ways that people negotiate their environments. It is our position that "disabilities" are constructed as abnormal and that this language continues to constitute a group of people as "less than" or "unable" as opposed to appreciating varying abilities as components of diversity on campus, such as race, gender, social class, and sexual orientation.

Ally: A person who works in a helpful capacity toward another. This book specifically discusses the role TAs can play as allies to LGBT students and colleagues by supporting and honoring sexual and gender diversity, challenging homophobic and heterosexist remarks and behaviors, and by exploring and understanding issues related to the LGBT community as part of responsible teaching.

Binary gender system: The socially constructed idea that there are two distinct, and opposite, genders in our culture: male and female. People who do not "fit" within one category or the other are erased by this understanding of gender.

Bisexual: A person who has significant emotional, sexual, and/or romantic attractions to both men and women.

Class, Social Class: "Class" usually refers to social stratum whose members share certain social, economic, and cultural characteristics. In other words, class is usually related to income, wealth, education, occupational prestige, and the privileges that accompany these hierarchical statuses. Social class standing intersects with sexuality and gender identity (as well as race, ability, religion, and nationality) in complicated ways.

183

Closet, Closeted, or being "in the closet:" The closet is commonly referred to by LGBT people as the state of hiding or concealing one's LGBT-identity and/or behavior from others, and sometimes even from oneself. The origin comes from an old drag phrase, "you can only tell he's gay by the female clothes in his closet."

Coming out, Coming out of the closet: The process of disclosing one's LGBT identity and/or behavior. Coming out can be a lifelong process of self-acceptance.

Coming Out Week: A week of pro-gay activities, often hosted on college campuses by LGBT student groups, to celebrate the LGBT community and increase its visibility.

Drag: The act of dressing in clothing that is commonly associated with the opposite gender. In drag shows, drag queens are men who dress and perform as women and drag kings are females who dress and perform as men.

Dyke: Once a derogatory slur for lesbians, but is now frequently reclaimed by some lesbians as a term of pride.

Fag(got): A derogatory slur for gay men, but has been reclaimed by some gay men as a term of pride.

Gay: Oftentimes "gay" is used as an adjective to refer to all people, regardless of gender, who have their primary emotional, sexual, and/or romantic attractions to people of the same sex/gender. However, when used as a noun, "gay" usually refers to gay men (i.e. men who have significant emotional, sexual and/or romantic attractions to other men).

Gender: While many people believe that the sex differences (i.e. anatomical, genetic, and hormonal differences) between men and women are biological, gender is considered the social concept by which particular characteristics construct men and women as "masculine" and "feminine." [Although, not everyone believes that sex is 100% biological, either!] People are socialized into behaving appropriately for their sex based on the culture and historical time period in which they live. Gender is often considered a social institution in our culture since it shapes our desires, behaviors, and identities so profoundly and is intimately related to power dynamics between men and women. Please see "(Trans)Gendering the Classroom," by Rob S. Pusch, for a more complex discussion of gender.

Gender Expression: The external representation of one's gender identity, usually expressed through "feminine" or "masculine" behavior, clothing, voice inflection, body adornment, and behaviors, etc. Typically, people who identify as transgender work to make their gender expression match their gender identity and not their "biological" sex. [Many people who identify as transgender resist the two-gender binary system altogether by refusing to be categorized as either a man or woman.]

Gender Identity: One's personal sense of being a man or woman; the name one uses to refer to his/her gender. For transgender people, their "biological" sex does not match their own gender identity.

Hegemony, hegemonic: A term developed by Italian Marxist theorist Antonio Gramsci to refer to the process by which those in power secure the consent of their "subordinates" by making their position/power seem natural and normal through the use of pleasure, fascination, humor, etc. In other words, this is not a type of power that works through overt force; instead, hegemony seduces us into believing that things are the way they are because, "they're supposed to be." For example, the idea that men and women should only be attracted to members of the opposite gender is a hegemonic belief system.

Heteronormativity: A concept used to describe how many social institutions and social policies reinforce the belief that human beings fall into two distinct and complementary categories, male and female, and the subsequent belief that those genders ought to fulfill complementary roles—that is, among others, that sexual relationships ought to exist only between males and females. To describe a social institution as heteronormative means that it has visible or hidden norms, some of which are viewed as normal only for males and others which are seen as normal only for females. Its purpose, as with many critical terms, is to help identify voices that have "fallen through the cracks" and who do not feel that they have an adequate means of expressing themselves within the current social worldview. Please see "Heteronormativity and Teaching at Syracuse University," by Susan Adams, for a more complete discussion of this term.

Heterosexism: An "ism" represents a system, ideology, or theory that includes a basis for privileging, or rewarding, certain groups over others on the basis of a particular characteristic. Heterosexism refers to the dominant cultural belief that heterosexuality is the one "normal" and "right" sexuality for all people. Heterosexism, therefore, influences the fact that LGBT people often experience prejudice and discrimination in many forms, but it also impacts non-LGBT people by defining a very narrow range of acceptable behaviors and identities.

Heterosexual: A person who has significant emotional, sexual, and/or romantic attractions to members of the opposite sex/gender.

Homophobia: While a strict translation refers to the fear and hatred of "homosexuals," homophobia encompasses a much broader definition by also incorporating the discomfort and dislike that people may feel toward LGBT people, the belief that LGBT people do not deserve the same rights and opportunities as people who aren't LGBT, and any language or practice that supports these ideologies, such as using derogatory slurs (even in jest).

Homosexual: A person who has significant emotional, sexual, and/or romantic attractions to members of the same sex. This term developed out of the medical literature and is not usually the preferred way most LGBT people refer to themselves or others.

Intersex: A term used to describe the occurrence of a person born with both male and female anatomical/physiological characteristics (which can occur in various combinations), or when a person's genitalia is biologically ambiguous. This happens more than you think, but doctors usually make a decision to surgically alter a child's genitalia at a very young age. Surgical alteration of genitalia to make an individual "fit" either a male or female sex category has led some theorists to argue that sex categories are not just biological; they are, in fact, socially- as well as biologically-constructed.

LGBT: An acronym for the identities Lesbian, Gay Men, Bisexual, and Transgender. At times, "Q" is added to refer to those who identify as Queer and/or Questioning (as in questioning their sexual identity). Also, sometimes "A" is added to refer to people who identify as LGBT Allies.

Lesbian: A woman who has significant emotional, sexual, and/or romantic attractions to other women. Also, a woman who is "woman-identified."

Pass: LGB people are said to "pass" when their LGB identity is not publicly exposed, i.e., they can "pass" as straight. Transgender people are said to "pass" when they can successfully live as their chosen gender.

Queer: This word emerged in the mid-to-late 1980s in order to reclaim a pejorative term that was once used to disparage LGBT people. Today, "queer" is used in many different ways. Some people use "queer" as an all-inclusive term to refer to anyone who is not heterosexual (i.e. all LGBT people). However, the term is also used in a highly political way by some non-straights to refer to their sexuality and/or progressive ideologies that reject compulsory heterosexuality and the practices that are often associated with it, i.e. these people identify as "queer" to mark their counter-hegemonic/anti-mainstream lifestyles. Queer Theory is a body of literature that has developed from this latter definition in order to contest the widespread beliefs related to our current understandings of sexuality.

Race: Socially constructed categories often related to ethnicity and perceived skin color. Like gender, race involves a complex web of social meanings but should be understood as a social structure that is intimately related to privileges in our culture. Race intersects with sexuality and gender (as well as ability, religion, social class, and nationality) in complicated ways.

Rainbow Flag, Pride Flag: A symbol of the LGBT community that denotes the unity and diversity that is present within it. The colors red, orange, yellow, green, blue, and purple are striped across its cloth.

Sexual Identity: One's personal sense of sexual orientation; the names people use to refer to their sexual orientation, i.e. lesbian, bisexual, gay, queer, questioning, etc.

Sexual Orientation: The favored term (as opposed to "sexual preference") used when referring to an individual's emotional, sexual, and/or romantic attractions to the same and/or opposite sex/gender, including LGB and heterosexual orientations. When sexual orientation is used just to describe LGBT people, this makes the sexual orientation of heterosexuals invisible.

Straight: Another word for heterosexual.

Transgender: An umbrella term for people whose gender identity and/or gender expression differs from the sex they were assigned at birth including, but not limited to, transsexuals, intersex people, and cross-dressers. Please see "(Trans) Gendering the Classroom, by Rob S. Pusch, for a more complex discussion of this term.

Transition: The complex process of altering one's gender. Transition often includes changing one's legal name, coming out to friends and family as transgender, and sometimes taking forms of hormone therapy and genital alteration.

Compiled by Kathleen Farrell

>>contributors

Kathleen Farrell is a doctoral candidate in the Department of Sociology as well as a Fellow of the Center for the Study of Popular Television in Newhouse and a 2004 recipient of the Graduate School's Outstanding TA Award. Kathleen's work primarily addresses the sociology of gender and sexuality, cultural studies, queer theory, and popular culture. She is currently on a fellowship from the sociology department to complete her dissertation—a study of television industry professionals and their work to increase and enrich representations of LGBT people on tv.

Nisha Gupta received her Ph.D. in Cultural Foundations of Education from Syracuse University in 2005. She teaches courses in Foundations of Education and Women's Studies. She served as a Teaching Fellow for the TA program at Syracuse University and was awarded the Graduate School's Outstanding TA Award in 2003. Her research interests in feminist epistemologies and multiple conceptions of the idea of multicultural education are reflected in her teaching interests in enhancing interdisciplinary and multiple teaching/learning styles.

Mary Queen is an assistant professor of English and Comparative Literatures at American University in Kuwait. She earned her Ph.D. in Composition and Cultural Rhetoric from Syracuse University in 2005. Her research focuses on rhetorical practices of transnational feminist and sexual minority social movements in digital environments.

>>editors

Susan M. Adams is a doctoral candidate in Composition and Cultural Rhetoric at Syracuse University. She enjoys teaching writing and working with SU's undergraduate students. Susan's research focuses on queer and feminist theories, with a particular focus on rhetorical negotiations of subjectivity and identity by actress/writers of the mid-19th century.

Ahoura Afshar is a Ph.D. student in Political Science at Syracuse University, with a master's degree in Human Rights from the London School of Economics. His main academic interests are human rights and international law.

Dean Allbritton recently graduated from Syracuse University with a master's degree in Spanish Literature and Language. His thesis dealt with the advent of queer literature in contemporary Spanish novels; he currently resides in Spain collecting further information for his future doctoral work and having many Spanish parties.

Katrina Arndt is a doctoral student and instructor in the School of Education. Her personal experiences inform her understanding of LGBT pedagogy, and she hopes all classrooms can be safe and welcoming places for all students.

Andrew Augeri graduated from Syracuse University in 2003, concentrating on marketing and analysis of television, film and advertising. Designing since 1997, he has created various marketing projects across campus for the Writing Program, the Counseling Center, the Center for Career Services, and the LGBT Resource Center.

Camille Baker, a sophomore Sociology and Graphic Arts major originally from Albuquerque, New Mexico, came to Syracuse University originally to study Public Communications. She now is interested in studying interactions among racial minority groups along with her communications studies. After graduating she plans on attending graduate school for Sociology.

contributors

Payal Banerjee is a doctoral student in Sociology. Her dissertation is about Indian immigrant information technology workers in the U.S. Payal has taught Social Problems and Sociology of Sex and Gender at the undergraduate level, where she has employed intersectional and transnational frameworks in building the courses.

Eldar Beiseitov is a doctoral candidate in the Department of Economics specializing in public finance and international economics. Eldar served as a TA, taught classes independently, and worked for the New York State Tax Study. Recently, Eldar helped in organizing the university forum on marriage equality, and the Reel Queer Film Festival, and has received the Foundation Award for his contributions to SU's LGBT community.

Jeremy Brunson is originally from Arizona. He and his partner of 10 years relocated to Syracuse so that Jeremy could earn a Ph.D. in Sociology and Disability Studies.

Rachel Burgess is a professional writing instructor (code for adjunct) in the Writing Program at Syracuse University.

Paul Butler completed his Ph.D. in Composition and Cultural Rhetoric at Syracuse in August 2004. He is assistant professor of English at Montclair State University in Montclair, New Jersey.

Kelly Concannon is a second year Ph.D. candidate in Composition and Cultural Rhetoric at Syracuse University. She taught composition at Illinois State University, Heartland Community College, and currently teaches both WRT 105 and 205 at Syracuse University. She is interested in feminist theory and feminist pedagogies, LGBT pedagogy and practice, and collaborative teaching/research methods.

Melissa Conroy is a Ph.D. candidate in Syracuse's Department of Religion. She will be joining Muskingum College's Department of Philosophy and Religion this fall in New Concord, Ohio. Her interests include religion and gender, popular culture, and cinema as well as psychoanalytic theory.

Nicole Lorene Dimetman came to the Maxwell School of Citizenship and Public Affairs on a Syracuse Graduate Scholarship. As a senior Political Science major at the University of Texas at San Antonio, she focused on civil liberties and homosexuality. She has continued this focus by studying the economic effects of the military's "Don't Ask, Don't Tell" policy. Nicole will continue her studies at the University of Texas Law School in the fall.

Tom Dunn is a graduate student and teaching assistant in the Department of Communication and Rhetorical Studies. His academic interests include the rhetorical creation of queer public sphere, queer public memory, and the rhetoric of the LGBT rights movement. Tom also serves as co-facilitator of Open Doors, the queer graduate student organization.

Deborah Freund is Vice Chancellor for Academic Affairs and Provost of Syracuse University. She is responsible for the academic leadership of all schools, colleges, and support units. She also holds the position of Professor of Public Administration in the Maxwell School of Citizenship and Public Affairs. She came to Syracuse in 1999 from Indiana University-Bloomington.

Cyril Ghosh is a Ph.D. student in the Department of Political Science, Syracuse University.

Sidney (Skip) Greenblatt is the Assistant Director for Advising and Counseling at the Slutzker Center for International Services at Syracuse University. He is also an adjunct associate professor of Sociology. Skip is a specialist on contemporary Chinese society. He is fluent in Chinese (Mandarin dialect) and a member of the National Committee on U.S.-China Relations.

Patricia Hayes holds a Bachelor of Music degree in Music Therapy from Nazareth College of Rochester and a Master of Divinity degree from St. Bernard's School of Theology and Ministry. She currently works for the LGBT Resource Center at Syracuse University where she is pursuing a Master of Social Work degree. Prior to working at SU, Hayes was employed at the Gay Alliance of the Genesee Valley in Rochester, NY as their Youth Program Coordinator working with and on behalf of LGBTQ youth and their families.

Margaret Himley is Associate Professor of Writing and Rhetoric and Director of Undergraduate Studies in the Writing Program, where she is lead faculty on a large project called Writing and Diversity in a Globalized World. As co-chair of the Senate Committee on LGBT Concerns, she is happy to be collaborating with others in bringing LGBT scholarship, issues, and perspectives into the educational work of the university.

Adrea Jaehnig was hired as the Director of the LGBT Resource Center in October 2001. Prior to this position, Adrea was the Associate Director of the Office of Residence Life at Syracuse University. She is a member of the Chancellor's Diversity Advisory Board, the Student Affairs Diversity Advisory Board, the Syracuse Welcome/New Student Orientation, the Syracuse University Team Against Bias, the Syracuse Area Domestic Violence Coalition, the University Senate Committee on LGBT Concerns, and an executive committee member of the National Consortium of Directors of LGBT Resource Centers.

Gerry Lambert is a graduate student in the M.F.A. Program in Creative Writing. He also teaches Writing 105 and 205 in the Writing Program.

Huei-Hsuan Lin is a non tenure-track assistant professor of Cultural Foundations of Education at Syracuse University. Her teaching and research interests include feminist pedagogy, schooling for social justice, qualitative methodology, and ethnography of urban community activism.

Andrew S. London is an associate professor and the Director of Graduate Studies in the Sociology department and a senior research associate in the Center for Policy Research in the Maxwell School. His research focuses on the health, care, and well-being of stigmatized and vulnerable populations. He is the co-chair of the University Senate Committee on LGBT Concerns.

Aman Luthra is a graduate student in the departments of Geography (M.A.) and Public Administration (M.P.A.). Aman grew up in Delhi, India and completed his undergraduate degree in Environmental Studies at the University of Maine at Machias. His current research focuses on the links between landscape representation and development as a nationalist project in Bhutan.

Jonathan Massey teaches in the School of Architecture at Syracuse University. He holds a bachelor of arts and doctoral degrees from Princeton University, as well as a Master of Architecture degree from U.C.L.A. Prior to joining the Syracuse faculty, he practiced and taught in Los Angeles and New York.

Rachel Moran is a sophomore at Syracuse University. She is studying History and Women's Studies, and minoring in Creative Writing.

Adina Mulliken is a reference librarian and selector for Social Work and allied fields at Bird Library. She is currently working part time on a Master of Social Science degree at Syracuse University.

Rob Pusch completed his doctoral work in Instructional Design, Development, and Evaluation in May, 2003. Rob's research investigated transgender college students' perspectives of their own transgender identities, their understanding of the relationship between their bodies and their identities, and how they felt they fit within the larger LGBT community.

Kristenne Robison is a first year Ph.D. student in Sociology. She received a B.A. in Psychology and Nutrition from Baldwin-Wallace College in 1996 and an M.A. in Education from Ohio State University in 1999. Kristenne spent the past four years as the head volleyball coach and instructor in the Department of Athletics and Recreation at St. Lawrence University. Kristenne's research interests include inequality studies, sport sociology, domestic violence, gender issues, race theory, and Native American culture.

Elizabeth Sierra-Zarella, a third year Ph.D. student in Child and Family Studies, was born and raised in Wichita Falls, Texas. Her experiences as a first-generation college student from an impoverished family, a Hispanic woman with multiple disabilities, and a former teen mother on welfare have caused her to face oppression on many levels. As a result, she is committed to identifying and removing the societal barriers preventing people from reaching their highest potential. She currently resides in Camillus, NY, with her husband, Mark, and her daughter, Tabitha.

Brian Stout is a Broadcast Journalism major. He has created and continues to develop LGBT educational and outreach programs on campus. He is the brotherhood chair of his fraternity, Delta Lambda Phi, and outreach coordinator of Pride Union, Syracuse University's undergraduate organization for lesbian, gay, bisexual, transgendered, and straight-allied students.

Justin Welch, from Pittsburgh, PA, is a Public Relations major in the S.I. Newhouse School of Public Communications. His dedication to LGBT concerns and issues have led him to work at the LGBT Resource Center at Syracuse University, as well as involvement in Pride Union, the Team Against Bias and a number of university councils and committees concerning diversity and other student issues.

Jennifer Wingard is a Ph.D. student in the Composition and Cultural Rhetoric program. Her research interests trace how issues of race, class, and gender are named and controlled by social institutions, and how these controls affect how knowledges are produced and consumed in the university.